Graphic Organizers

Visual Strategies for Active Learning

by
Karen Bromley
Linda Irwin-DeVitis
Marcia Modlo

SCHOLASTIC
PROFESSIONAL BOOKS

New York • Toronto • London • Auckland • Sydney

Dedication and Acknowledgments

For: Irene, Dick, and Bob from KB
Dorothy, Edward, Joe, and Leigh from LI
Mamie, Moxie, Bob, and Garrett from MM

We are fortunate to have worked with many fine teachers and their students in the years before writing this book and during the course of the book's creation. We are grateful that many of these teachers and their students have allowed us to include their work and tell their stories here, for it is in the context of real and diverse classrooms that the rich potential of the graphic organizer can best be understood. We extend our sincere appreciation to all those teachers whose names appear here: Kim Ames, Elsa Bingel, Bonnie Slentz, Sara Brundage, Kathy Bucker, Pat Ciotoli, Kelly Haight, Virginia Hawkins, Gail Innerfield, Lucy Kelly, Jan Kemmery, Penelope Koval, Cathy Lynch, Doreen McSain, Colleen Murphy, Connie Moxley, Deborah Pease, Lynda Race, Judith Reed, Dana Roney-Naverz, Doreen Saar, Sheri Serfass, and Gerry Tastle.

ISBN 0-590-48928-3
Cover design by Vincent Ceci
Interior illustration by Drew Hires
Book design by Carmen Robert Sorvillo
Copyright © 1995 by Karen Bromley, Linda DeVitis,
and Marcia Modlo
Printed in USA
12 11 10 9 8 7 6 5 4 3 2   /5 9

Table of Contents

Introduction

This practical handbook demonstrates how to use a variety of graphic organizers for teaching and learning, for planning, instruction, and assessment in grades kindergarten through eight.

The graphic organizer is a visual representation of knowledge. Graphic organizers facilitate prereading, postreading, writing, reasoning, and discussion of print in all subjects. They represent knowledge from nonprint sources such as video, lecture, and audio. As you and your students create graphic organizers, you will use language in purposeful ways and learn from each other as you extend and refine your understandings of new concepts and ideas.

We want this book to be practical and easy to use across the curriculum. With this in mind, we include descriptions of lessons and units in which graphic organizers are used with all ages of students and in a variety of subjects, including science, mathematics, language arts, and social studies. The teachers, classrooms, and work described here are real; we address both the problems and successes related to the use of graphic organizers. This book is intended to encourage and support you as you use this strategy in your classroom and discover its potential as a learning tool for yourself and your students.

We believe so strongly in graphic organizers' effectiveness for organizing ideas and illustrating relationships that we used one to launch and guide our discussion of each chapter's contents. We discovered that talk and negotiation are critical for the creation of a graphic organizer that accurately represents both content and the views of three collaborators.

In writing this book we have learned much about the graphic organizer, more than any of us knew initially. We have learned much about each other as people, women, and educators. We have developed our friendships. We have built on our individual strengths, and we believe this book is much stronger because of our collaboration than if it had been single-authored. Each of us shared equally in its creation.

— KB, LI, MM

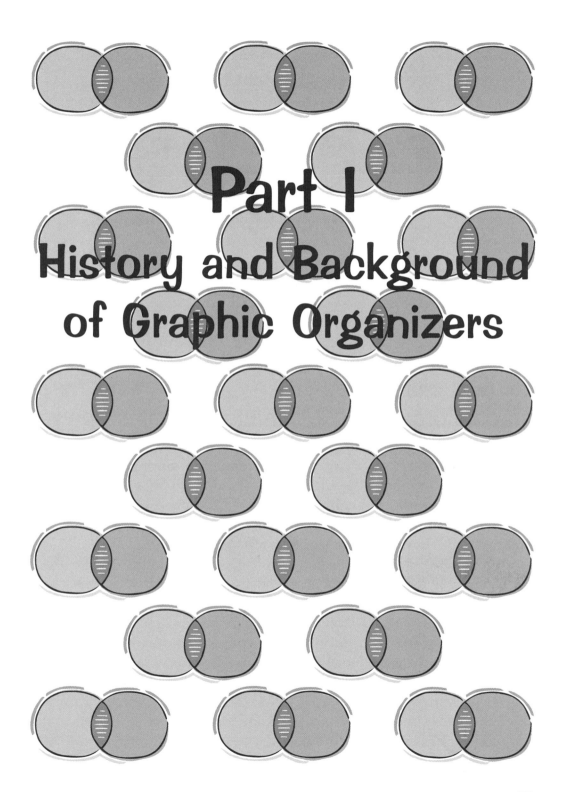

Part I
History and Background of Graphic Organizers

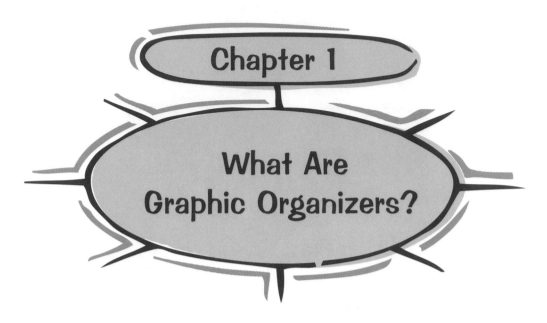

Chapter 1

What Are
Graphic Organizers?

Semantic map, structured overview, web, concept map, semantic organizer, story map, graphic organizer....No matter what the special name, a graphic organizer is a visual representation of knowledge. It is a way of structuring information, of arranging important aspects of a concept or topic into a pattern using labels. A graphic organizer promotes active learning. It exercises students' use of language as they read, talk, listen, think, and write. It requires students to engage with information and grapple with what they do and do not know. Last, a graphic organizer is a highly effective tool for improving social interaction because it facilitates group work between students and teachers and among collaborative peers.

Graphic organizers make visually explicit the organizational patterns of text. They can be enlisted to facilitate prereading, postreading, prewriting, revising, discussing, and reasoning. They can represent students' background knowledge and provide a framework for what is about to be learned, or can be used to organize and reflect on newly acquired knowledge. As teachers and students create graphic organizers together, they learn from each other as they extend their understandings of concepts. Through this collaborative activity, students learn how to organize their knowledge, and eventually can use the graphic organizer independently as a learning strategy. Because graphic organizers involve both visual and verbal information, they are beneficial for students with a wide variety of learning styles and ranges of ability.

● ● ● ● ● ● ● ● ● ● ● ● ● ● ● ● ●

What Is the Theory Behind Their Use?

Here are four important ideas from learning theory that underlie the use of graphic organizers:

1. When important information is isolated, we can see how concepts are connected, and this makes it more easily understood (Novak & Gowin, 1984). Omitting extraneous information and presenting only what is essential simplifies the learning task.
2. The mind arranges and stores information in an orderly fashion (Ausubel, 1968). New information about a concept is filed into an existing framework of categories called a schema that contains specific information about that concept (Rumelhart, 1980). So, when prior knowledge is retrieved, this schema provides a framework on which to attach new knowledge.

> **Graphic organizers make visually explicit the organizational patterns of text. They can be enlisted to facilitate prereading, postreading, prewriting, revising, discussing, and reasoning.**

3. A visual graphic containing key ideas and information is easier to remember than extended text, whether the text is visual or verbal. Vygotsky (1962) calls this graphic a semiotic mediator, a mental tool to help the learner remember.

4. The use of both visual and verbal language to create graphic organizers results in active learning. When print and spoken language are used together, the learner is engaged through listening, speaking, reading, writing, and thinking, and this reinforcement aids meaningful learning.

● ● ● ● ● ● ● ● ● ● ● ● ● ● ● ●

What Does the Research Say?

Creating graphic organizers to illustrate the organization of ideas and information aids comprehension and learning (Flood & Lapp, 1988; Heimlich & Pittelman, 1986). Most of the research examines the use of graphic organizers in reading. Few studies examine their use with either discussion or writing, suggesting these as important areas for future investigation.

Dunston (1992) reviewed ten years of research on the use of graphic organizers to aid the comprehension of content area texts. Her findings were similar to those of Moore and Readance (1984) who completed a similar review of earlier research. Dunston found

that when presented before reading to elementary students, graphic organizers aid comprehension and recall of information. She also discovered that when students construct graphic organizers after reading, elementary students' recall improves and secondary students' scores on vocabulary and comprehension improve. Dunston found that the effects of graphic organizers are greatest when students have in-depth instruction and training in their use and when students construct graphic organizers themselves.

So, both theory and research support the use of the graphic organizer as an active learning strategy. Now let's look at how they can be used to represent knowledge.

● ● ● ● ● ● ● ● ● ● ● ● ● ● ● ●

How Is Knowledge Organized?

Traditionally, graphic organizers have been used by content area teachers to represent patterns of text organization. Typically, graphic organizers are used to show the structure of information in material from a science or social studies book. But virtually all

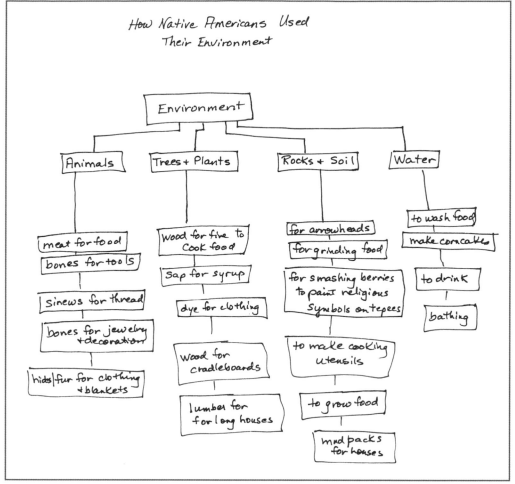

How Native Americans Used Their Environment

Environment
- Animals
  - meat for food
  - bones for tools
  - sinews for thread
  - bones for jewelry + decoration
  - hides/fur for clothing + blankets
- Trees + Plants
  - Wood for fire to cook food
  - Sap for syrup
  - dye for clothing
  - Wood for cradleboards
  - lumber for for long houses
- Rocks + Soil
  - for arrowheads
  - for grinding food
  - for smashing berries to paint religious symbols on tepees
  - to make cooking utensils
  - to grow food
  - mud packs for houses
- Water
  - to wash food
  - make corncakes
  - to drink
  - bathing

figure 1.1   A teacher and her students create a hierarchical organizer for "How Native Americans Used Their Environment."

sources of knowledge—not just print—contain meaning that can be represented in graphic organizers. For example, information and ideas presented through film, lecture, video, and discussion can be organized and depicted graphically. As elementary and secondary-school teachers use graphic organizers to help their students learn concepts and information, we encourage them to continually widen the arena of graphic organizer's use.

There are four basic patterns of knowledge organization: hierarchical, conceptual, sequential, and cyclical. Graphic organizers can be constructed for each of these four organizational patterns:

• **Hierarchical.** This pattern includes a main concept and the ranks, or levels, of subconcepts under it. Generalizations and classifications are examples of this type of linear organizer. For example, in Figure 1.1 a fourth grade teacher provided her students with the general idea of environment and the four subcategories, or aspects, of it. After students read appropriate historical fiction and the social studies text, the teacher worked with them to com-

plete the organizer, adding examples to each category of specific things the Native Americans used in order to survive.

• **Conceptual.** This pattern includes a central idea, category, or class with supporting facts such as characteristics or examples. Description, collection, problem/solution, and comparison/contrast are examples of this type of organizer.

The graphic organizer in Figure 1.2 shows how a class of fifth graders conceived of the integration of language arts. Through

figure 1.2   A fifth grade class's conceptual organizer for "Language."

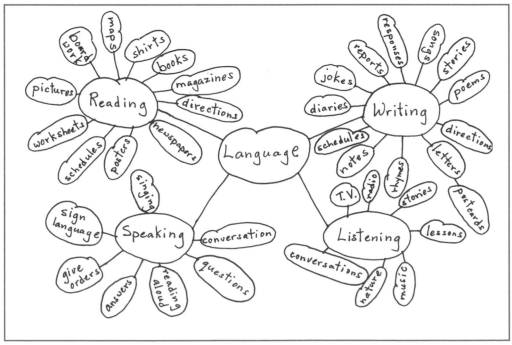

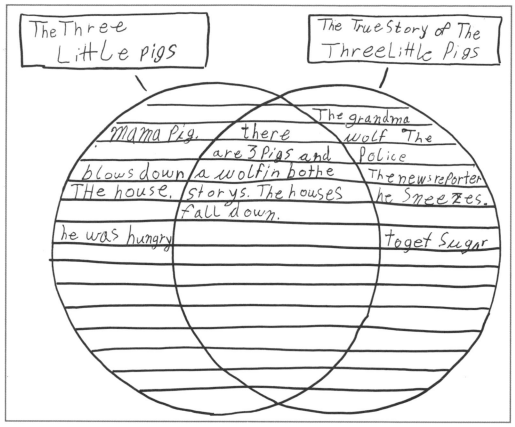

The Three Little pigs

The True Story of The Three Little Pigs

mama Pig.

there are 3 Pigs and a wolf in bothe storys. The houses fall down.

The grandma wolf The Police The news reporter he sneezes.

blows down THe house.

he was hungry

to get Sugar

figure 1.3   Second graders' comparison/contrast organizer for two versions of "The Three Little Pigs."

discussion, Sara Brundage, their teacher, helped the students identify language as the central ingredient in communication. Then they identified listening, speaking, reading, and writing as distinct language processes and brainstormed a range of activities in which they hoped to be engaged during the year that would allow them to develop each language process.

A Venn diagram is another example of a conceptual organizer. This diagram of two overlapping circles is often used to represent information that is being compared and contrasted. After reading two versions of the "Three Little Pigs," second graders Liam and Bobby talked about the similarities and differences in the stories. Then they created a Venn diagram to represent their discussion

(Figure 1.3). The diagram provided them with notes to refer to as they reported their information to their group.

• **Sequential.** This pattern, as the name suggests, arranges events in a chronological order. They are useful in organizing events that have a specific beginning and end into cause/effect, chronology, process/product, or problem/solution. Sequential patterns are usually linear; a time line is a classic example. Figure 1.4 shows a sequential organizer for *The Polar Express* by Chris Van Allsburg (Houghton Mifflin, 1986) created by third graders. After reading this book about the magic of Christmas and a young boy's trip to the North Pole, students discussed it and then recounted the boy's trip with this organizer. In Figure 1.5, students and their teachers use a sequential organiz-

figure 1.4   Third graders sequence the events in *The Polar Express* by Chris Van Allsburg.

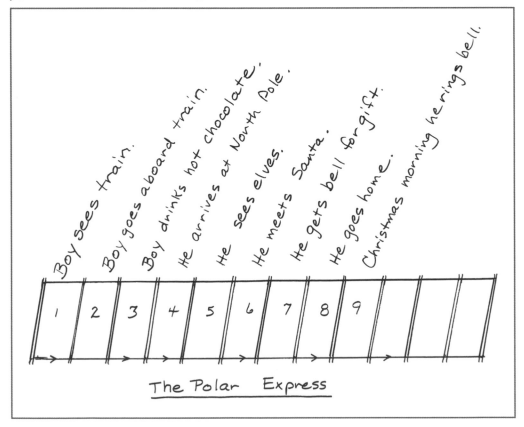

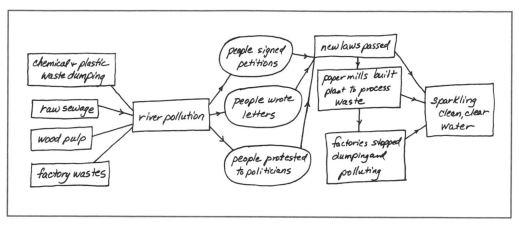

figure 1.5   Students use this sequential organizer to zero in on problem solving in *A River Ran Wild* by Lynne Cherry.

figure 1.6   The balance of nature is depicted in this cyclical organizer for *The Old Ladies Who Loved Cats* by Carol Greene.

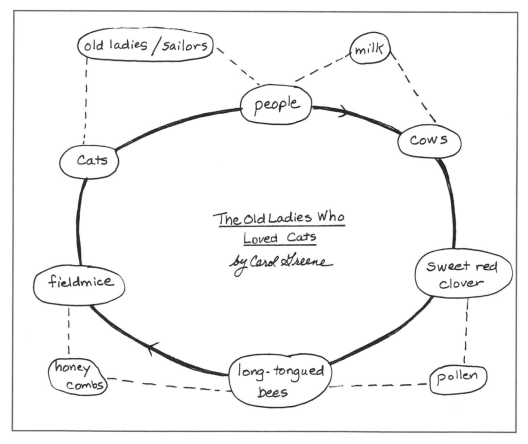

er to depict a problem and its solution. After reading *A River Ran Wild* by Lynne Cherry (Harcourt, 1992), these fourth graders showed the events that caused pollution in the Nashua River and the events that helped solve the problem.

• **Cyclical.** This pattern includes a series of events within a process in a circular formation. In a cyclical pattern there is no beginning or end, just a continuous sequence of events. This type of organizer depicts information in a series, succession, or cycle. Figure 1.6 shows a graphic organizer created by a teacher and her students to represent the story *The Old Ladies Who Loved Cats* by Carol Greene (Harper, 1991). Identifying the life cycle on this imaginary island off the northeastern coast of the United States helped reinforce the notion of life cycles for these students.

• • • • • • • • • • • • • • • • • •

What Are the Benefits of Graphic Organizers?

While graphic organizers aid learning for all students, they are especially appropriate for students with language differences and processing difficulties. The graphic organizer highlights key vocabulary, provides an organized visual display of knowledge, and facilitates discussion and sharing of ideas and information. It requires the integration of language and thinking as students with different learning styles or rates of learning distill information into more easily digestible pieces.

Teachers at all grade levels use graphic organizers for many reasons and in a variety of ways. Some of the most important reasons for using graphic organizers are outlined below.

• **Focus attention on key elements.** To create a graphic organizer, both teachers and students pay close attention to important concepts and ideas. In order to create a graphic organizer, students must be able to distinguish among "big ideas," "little ideas," and supporting details.

• **Help integrate prior knowledge with new knowledge.** Graphic organizers can represent an individual's background knowledge and provide a framework for the addition of new

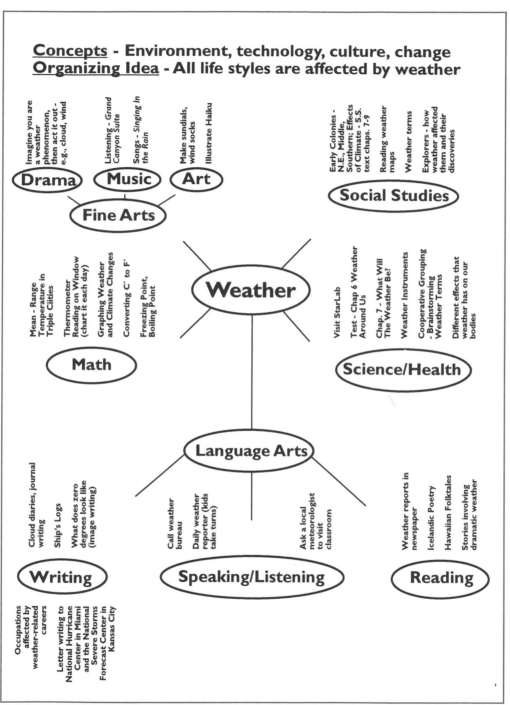

Concepts - Environment, technology, culture, change
Organizing Idea - All life styles are affected by weather

Drama
- Imagine you are a weather phenomenon, then act it out - e.g., cloud, wind

Music
- Listening - *Grand Canyon Suite*
- Songs - *Singing In the Rain*

Art
- Make sundials, wind socks
- Illustrate Haiku

Fine Arts

Social Studies
- Early Colonies - N.E, Middle, Southern; Effects of Climate - S.S. text chaps. 7-9
- Reading weather maps
- Weather terms
- Explorers - how weather affected them and their discoveries

Weather

Math
- Mean - Range Temperature in Triple Cities
- Thermometer Reading on Window (chart it each day)
- Graphing Weather and Climate Changes
- Converting C° to F°
- Freezing Point, Boiling Point

Science/Health
- Visit StarLab
- Test - Chap 6 Weather Around Us
- Chap. 7 - What Will The Weather Be?
- Weather Instruments
- Cooperative Grouping - Brainstorming Weather Terms
- Different effects that weather has on our bodies

Language Arts

Writing
- Cloud diaries, journal writing
- Ship's Logs
- What does zero degrees look like (image writing)
- Occupations affected by weather-related careers
- Letter writing to National Hurricane Center in Miami and the National Severe Storms Forecast Center in Kansas City

Speaking/Listening
- Call weather bureau
- Daily weather reporter (kids take turns)
- Ask a local meteorologist to visit classroom

Reading
- Weather reports in newspaper
- Icelandic Poetry
- Hawaiian Folktales
- Stories involving dramatic weather

figure 1.7   A graphic organizer constructed by a third grade teacher to help him plan for instruction in science.

knowledge. When we can "hook" new information to what is already known, learning the new information is easier and makes sense.

• **Enhance concept development.** Graphic organizers represent key ideas with appropriate vocabulary and help students see the attributes of a concept. Graphic organizers aid comprehension and learning because they use vocabulary that explains, clarifies, and illustrates the informational structure of the concept.

• **Enrich reading, writing, and thinking.** Students extend their reading, writing and thinking as they create graphic organizers. When students create and discuss a graphic representation of information, they reread, talk, reason, and see relationships that were not obvious before.

• **Aid writing by supporting planning and revising.** Graphic organizers—especially conceptual organizers because they are nonlinear and recursive—are effective ways to brainstorm, plan, and organize writing. The writer adds ideas to an organizer as they occur and decides on the order to use in writing. The graphic organizer supports revision as well, as the writer can refer to it to see what may have been inadvertently omitted.

• **Promote focused discussion.** As students create graphic organizers, they negotiate with one another to construct shared meanings. They use language in authentic ways to interpret, analyze, problem solve, predict, agree, disagree, cooperate, validate, connect, and extend their learning about a specific topic or concept.

• **Assist instructional planning.** Teachers who use graphic organizers in planning for instruction find them invaluable. The graphic organizer in Figure 1.7 gives a pictorial overview of the key elements a third grade teacher identified as important to include in her science unit on weather. The graphic organizer provides a skeletal structure for exploration of a theme, topic, or piece of literature before teaching and a way to add information and ideas as the unit is taught to improve future instruction.

• **Serve as an assessment and evaluation tool.** The graphic organizer can be used as one means of assessing student learning. Rather than, or along with, writing an essay, some teachers give students the option of creating a graphic organizer to show what they learned. When graphic organizers are used in this way, they also become good sources of information for the teacher to guide future instruction.

● ●

References

Ausubel, D.P. (1968). *Educational Psychology: A Cognitive View*. New York: Holt.

Dunston, P.J. (1992). "A Critique of Graphic Organizer Research." *Reading Research and Instruction*, 31 (2), 57-65.

Flood, J., & Lapp, D. (1988). "Conceptual Mapping Strategies for Understanding Information Texts. *The Reading Teacher*, 41 (8), 780-783.

Heimlich, J.E., & Pittelman, S.D. (1986). *Semantic Mapping: Classroom Applications*. Newark, DE: International Reading Association.

Moore, D.W., & Readance, J.E. (1984). "A Quantitative and Qualitative Review of Graphic Organizer Research." *Journal of Educational Research*, 78, 11-17.

Novak, J.D., & Gowin, D.B. (1984). *Learning How To Learn*. New York: Cambridge University Press.

Rumelhart, D.E. (1980). "Schemata: The Building Blocks of Cognition." In R.J. Spiro, B.C. Bruce and W.F. Brewer (Eds.), *Theoretical Issues in Reading Comprehension*, 33-58. Hillsdale, NJ: Erlbaum.

Vygotsky, L.S. (1962). *Thought and Language*. Cambridge, MA: MIT Press.

Further Reading

Cassidy, J. (1991). "Using Graphic Organizers to Develop Critical Thinking." *Gifted Child Today*,   12 (6), 34-36.

Sorenson, S. (1991). *Working with Special Students in English/Language Arts.* Bloomington, IN: Eric Clearinghouse on Reading and Communication Skills.

Questions & Answers

I thought graphic organizers were most appropriate for secondary students. Can elementary-school age children really deal with graphic organizers?

Children are ready for graphic organizers as soon as they can deal with similarities, differences and categories. For very young children, you can use visual aides such as pictures or felt-board pieces to demonstrate these concepts. As your children begin to read, you can serve as a "scribe" by recording their ideas in a graphic organizer format. Then ask your children to make connections among the ideas with your help. You need to be aware that your students' success with graphic organizers will vary according to their developmental level, interests and abilities.

Is this strategy only for students who are visual learners?

No. While graphic organizers are holistic visual representations of concepts and facts, they are useful learning tools for students who are not primarily visual learners. However, these students need opportunities to develop their ability to learn using all their senses—visual, auditory, kinesthetic, and tactile. Even if students are not primarily visual learners, they can still benefit from the process of developing graphic organizers and the activities that accompany it, i.e., discussing, problem-solving, researching, and organizing.

Students from diverse cultures may bring different schema to the construction of graphic organizers. It is important for teachers and students to be accepting of all students' contributions.

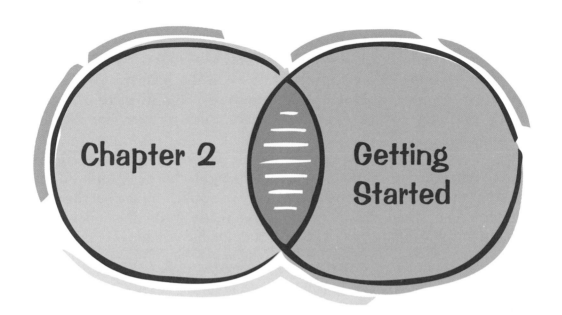

Chapter 2 — Getting Started

Graphic organizers can be constructed on the chalkboard, overhead projector, or chart paper. The chalkboard is accessible to you and your students, while the overhead projector has the advantage of allowing you (or a student) to face the class while creating the organizer. Of course, the overhead transparency can then be photocopied for the class. Chart paper is large and accessible and has the added benefit of being a permanent copy that can be posted for future reference.

You can even create graphic organizers with students who are not yet reading by using pictures rather than words. Gail Innerfield created the organizer in Figure 2.1 to guide discussion of *Where the Wild Things Are* by Maurice Sendak (Harper & Row, 1963). You can use different colors to represent different categories of information or to represent the contributions of individual students.

Organizers that are generated by a group or by the entire class can be reproduced on standard-size paper and photocopied so that each student has his or her own copy for later study or review. Using computers with graphic capabilities can add another dimension to organizers. Software is available at a number of levels of sophistication. Figure 2.2 is an example of a computer-designed graphic organizer on using computers to create graphic organizers.

It's best if you lead the initial activities using graphic organizers until students get the hang of them. Also, when you are introducing graphic organizers to your students, use one that is based upon a topic with which your students are familiar.

In the primary grades this might be a favorite picture book or topics, such as pets, families, or seasons.

For intermediate students, you might choose a topic in science or social studies that the class has already studied, or a book that students have read recently.

figure 2.1   Gail Innerfield's graphic organizer for *Where the Wild Things Are.*

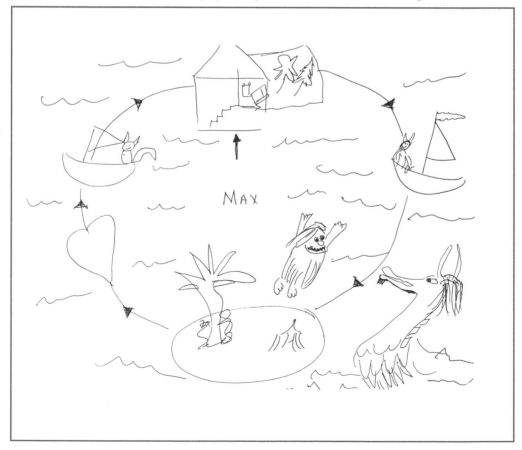

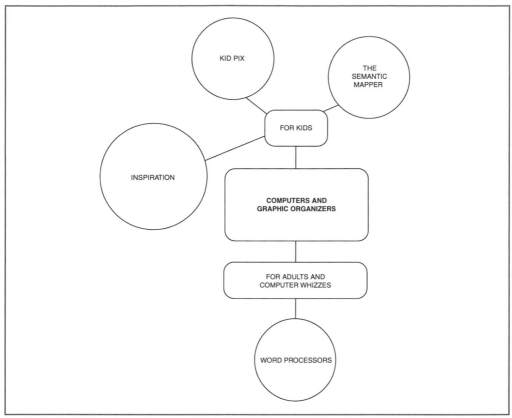

figure 2.2   A graphic organizer on computer software used in creating graphic organizers.

Using Graphic Organizers to Activate and Develop Prior Knowledge

A good way to begin generating graphic organizers is to use one in brainstorming. The organizer is used to visually represent a concept and the background knowledge (schema) that students already possess about that concept. The graphic organizer in Figure 2.3 shows the collective background knowledge generated by Sally Neaves's fourth sgrade students about jaguars.

Sally began by putting the word *jaguar* in a rectangle in the center of an overhead transparency. She asked her students to share what they knew about jaguars and categorized the information her students generated about the animal into three general areas—family life, physical characteristics, and habits. Sally encouraged a dialogue and elaboration of the students' answers by asking probing questions. Students extended and refined their knowledge of jaguars through both the discussion and the visual representation of their collective background knowledge.

As in all activities designed to activate prior knowledge, students will benefit from hearing what others have to say. The graphic organizers have the additional advantage of recording the shared information permanently in visual form. This is particularly beneficial for students who are primarily visual learners, as well as for those who require more time to process information.

When using the graphic organizer to record a brainstorming activity, accept all ideas. The graphic organizer can be modified by students after reading or research to reflect additional learning and to correct misconceptions. In some cases students will want to generate a new web when

figure 2.3   The initial graphic organizer constructed by Sally Neaves's fourth graders on the topic of jaguars.

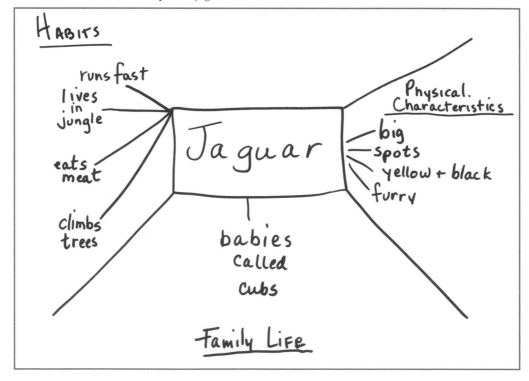

they reconceptualize the information. Figure 2.4 (pg. 24) shows the modifications that Sally's fourth grade class made after reading about jaguars.

After reading about jaguars, Zachary, the student who had volunteered in the initial discussion that jaguars had spots, said that spots should be changed to black all over. Sally used one color to write the information generated before reading and another color to write information or corrections made after reading. This helped students understand their new learning about jaguars and how it related to what they already knew.

● ● ● ● ● ● ● ● ● ● ● ● ● ● ●

Using Graphic Organizers to Highlight Knowledge Organization

When using graphic organizers to highlight the organization of knowledge, you may want to begin with a completed graphic organizer. Figure 2.5 (pg. 24) was constructed by fifth grade teacher Ed Boyd as a prereading activity for his lesson on the rain cycle.

Ed's goal was to activate his students' background knowledge about rain and to create interest in the topic. By highlighting the cyclical nature of the process, Ed made it easier for his students to understand the relationships between evaporation and condensation, the role of the sun, and clouds. So, the graphic organizer highlighted the organization of knowledge and made the relationships between concepts and processes visually explicit.

When students are familiar with completed graphic organizers, you might challenge them with a partially completed one. Marty McCampbell, a first grade teacher, invited her students to research the information needed to complete Figure 2.6 (pg. 25) as part of a social studies unit. In order to complete the organizer, Marty's students needed to become actively engaged with the knowledge and the concepts and the relationships it represents.

As students develop proficiency with this strategy, it is beneficial for them to try using a blank organizer (see Appendix B). Examining the information to determine the appropriate subcategories and their descriptors and

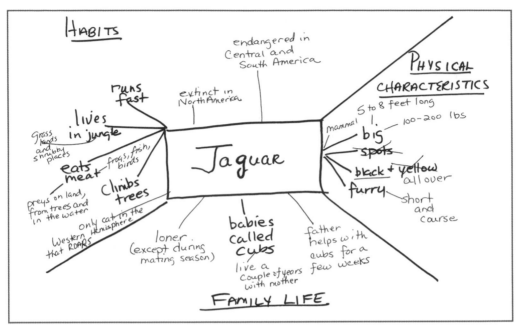

図 *figure 2.4* Modified graphic organizer constructed by Sally Neaves's fourth graders after reading about jaguars.

figure 2.5 Ed Boyd's cyclical graphic organizer on the rain cycle.

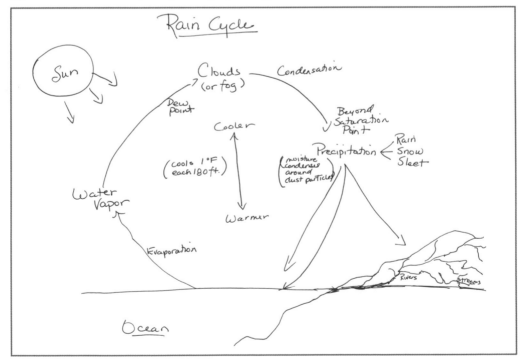

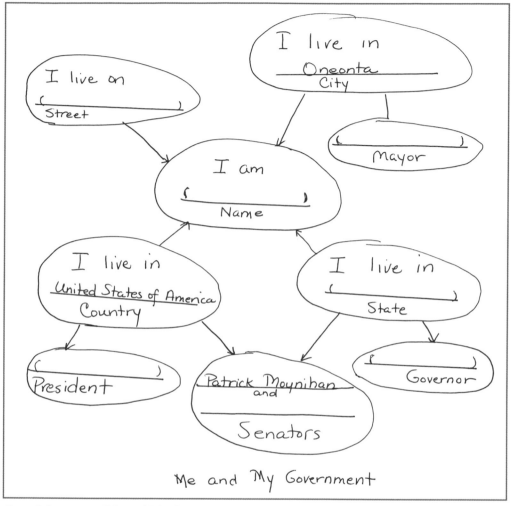

figure 2.6   "Me and My Government" organizer created and partially completed by first grade teacher Marty McCampbell.

deciding which type of organizer is most appropriate requires students to grapple with the organization of knowledge. In some cases the students will find they need to create their own structure; that is, they will construct the graphic organizer independently.

Helping Students Use Graphic Organizers Independently

The most effective way to guide students to use graphic organizers on their own is by constantly modeling the process of constructing one. Explain the process you go through in creating the organizer; this "think aloud" strategy (Davey, 1983) provides valuable modeling for your students. Discuss the way in which you determine the central concept

> **Students who understand how to create a graphic organizer have a new and valuable tool for planning, understanding, remembering, and assessing knowledge.**

and the key relationships. It helps students tremendously when you show the "mistakes" and "alterations" you make as you generate and revise your organizer. Through this candid demonstration students can better understand the thinking, rethinking, hypothesizing, and decision making that go into creating a graphic organizer.

By independently generating the structure of a graphic organizer, students demonstrate their depth of understanding of a concept as well as their command of the process of organizing knowledge. Students who understand how to create a graphic organizer have a new and valuable tool for planning, understanding, remembering, and assessing knowledge.

● ● ● ● ● ● ● ● ● ● ● ● ● ● ● ●

Promoting Critical Thinking

There are many ways you can use graphic organizers to promote critical thinking. For example, you can present two graphic organizers depicting the same information and have students debate and cite evidence to support which organizer is more effective. Or, you can use a Venn diagram to have students discover the similarities and differences between two stories. Another good critical-thinking activity is to have students examine a graphic organizer to determine the information that is not there. Students can then read or research to find the missing information and add it to the organizer. Encourage students to think about and discuss the patterns of knowledge organization discussed in Chapter 1 (hierarchical, conceptual, sequential, and cyclical) and the types of graphic organizers that are most common in science, history, literature, health, and other subjects.

● ● ● ● ● ● ● ● ● ● ● ● ● ● ● ● ●

Graphic Organizers and Individual Learning Styles

Teachers can help each student explore the value of the graphic organizer by having students:

• Examine the use of graphic organizers in their texts and tradebooks. As students take note of how authors use graphic organizers, they will understand the many applications of graphic organizers.

• Consider when and how to use graphic organizers in their learning. Some students will find that they benefit most from constructing their own organizer; others will prefer to use organizers that appear in their textbooks or that were created by their teacher or classmates. Students often find that they prefer different types of organizers to serve a variety of purposes in their own learning.

• Experiment with graphic organizers, review questions, traditional outlines, summaries, and other study techniques to determine which is the most effective strategy for them. Until students compare the various study techniques, they will not really know which is most beneficial for them.

• Assess the value of graphic organizers in different situations and contexts.

You will know that your instruction has been successful when some of your students choose to use graphic organizers in their own brainstorming, prewriting, learning logs, note-taking and studying, and test taking.

● ● ● ● ● ● ● ● ● ● ● ● ● ● ● ● ●

Seven Key Points

The ability to understand, use, and create graphic organizers takes time to develop. Your students will need careful instruction and guidance as they explore this learning strategy. Using graphic organizers yourself is a good way to begin. It will be difficult to convince your students that graphic organizers have value for them if they do not see you use graphic organizers in your own learning and writing.

(Chapter 4 will present ideas for using graphic organizers in instructional planning and assessment.)

As you begin to use graphic organizers with your students, it is important to remember these seven key points:

1. The graphic organizer is a mental tool to aid comprehension, recall, and learning. Graphic organizers are not an end in themselves.
2. The process of creating, discussing, sharing, and evaluating a graphic organizer is more important than the organizer itself. Students learn from the active investigation and negotiation, or give and take, that accompanies the use of a graphic organizer.
3. A gradual transition from teacher-directed graphic organizer activities to independent use of graphic organizers is best. You will want your students to participate in learning activities that fall within their zone of proximal development, that is, the area in which they can function effectively with instruction (Vygotsky, 1962). Ultimately, the goal of instruction is to support students as they gradually become independent.
4. The discussion that accompanies the creation or interpretation of a graphic organizer is crucial to the learning process. According to Vygotsky (1962) learning is first, social; only after working with others does the student gain the ability to understand and apply learning independently.
5. There are many ways to represent the same information in a graphic organizer. There is no one right answer.
6. Some students will find graphic organizers more beneficial than others.
7. Encourage students to evaluate the benefits of graphic organizers in their own learning.

References

Davey, B. (1983). "Think aloud: Modeling the Cognitive Processes of Reading Comprehension." *Journal of Reading*, 27, (1), 44-47.

Vygotsky, L. (1962). *Thought and Language*. Cambridge, MA: MIT Press.

Questions & Answers

What about the student who is not motivated to use graphic organizers?

While the graphic organizer is an important strategy for all students to learn, it should be one of a repertoire of strategies at students' fingertips. Effective teachers provide a variety of instructional formats to meet the needs and interests of students in a variety of learning situations. Students should know how to use data charts, mnemonic devices, KWL charts, note taking techniques, and so on.

How do I deal with students who get "off topic" as they brainstorm ideas for a graphic organizer?

First, you can merely stop the process by calling "time-out." You can point out the central thought, idea, or topic and ask students to make sure their answers are related to it. Or, you can let the students decide, item-by-item if necessary, whether or not each part of the graphic organizer fits the topic or central idea. Second, you can assign a student the role of "checker" during the brainstorming process. One student's "job" therefore can be to assess the validity of brainstormed ideas and make a decision or request help if an idea does not seem to fit the central thought or topic. This role can be rotated among students each time brainstorming occurs.

What happens when cultural differences impact the way students respond to graphic organizers?

Students from diverse cultures may bring different schema to the construction of graphic organizers. It is important for teachers and students to be accepting of all students' contributions.

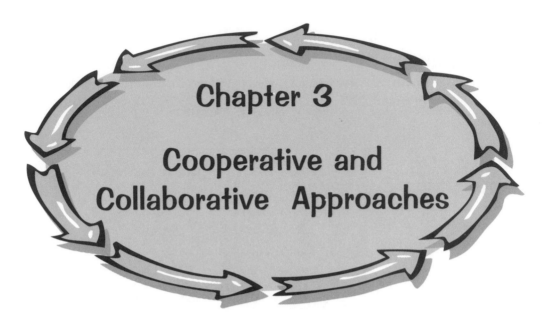

Chapter 3

Cooperative and
Collaborative Approaches

After several lessons using graphic organizers, a group of third grade students was asked, "How do graphic organizers help you learn?" They said:

- They help you learn faster and easier.
- Everything is connected.
- They help me learn more about a concept or a certain topic.
- You can just take a quick glance instead of reading a lot of paragraphs.

The setting in which these children learned to use graphic organizers was a collaborative classroom in which the class was exploring the topic of grasslands in social studies. The teacher, Sheri Serfass, encourages her students to learn by talking and interacting. She views collaboration as a generic term that means a community of learners working together in any joint intellectual activity.

Sheri organizes her class into heterogeneous groups of four or five students who work cooperatively on assigned tasks and activities for several weeks at a time. She defines cooperative learning as the instructional use of small groups of students working together to accomplish a common purpose. Sheri believes that cooperative learning maximizes student learning.

● ● ● ● ● ● ● ● ● ● ● ● ● ● ● ●

Social Skills

Cooperative learning provides Sheri's students with opportunities to develop social skills in a natural context. When her students create and use graphic organizers in cooperative groups, they better understand concepts and content, and their social skills grow. Sheri believes that cooperative learning fosters the following social skills:

• **Listening.** Students become active listeners who paraphrase and summarize each others' contributions and thoughts relating to the topic.

• **Speaking.** Students convey points fluently and in effective ways as they communicate, construct, and create.

• **Questioning.** Students learn to pose questions about content and process.

• **Turn-taking.** Students participate equally and accomplish their tasks. They learn to avoid monopolizing the conversation.

• **Providing positive and constructive feedback.** Students give positive and constructive feedback and encourage and praise each other. They learn to celebrate their accomplishments.

> **Students learn to nurture and support each other.**
> **They become more caring and openly helpful to each individual in the group.**

• **Respecting opinions.** Students learn to value and appreciate diversity, including each other's learning styles, race, and language. Students learn to nurture and support each other. They become more caring and openly helpful to each individual in the group.

As we are all aware, it is crucial to teach and model these social skills for children. These same skills make it easier for children to learn the strategy of developing graphic organizers together. The following sections describe how five third-grade students worked cooperatively to create graphic organizers.

● ● ● ● ● ● ● ● ● ● ● ● ● ● ● ●

A Collaborative Venture

As the third graders worked together to brainstorm and create a graphic organizer for the topic of grasslands, they used the social skills discussed previously. Their discussion allowed them to engage in shared meaning collaboration, negotiation, and problem solving. Of course, there is much overlapping among these categories.

First, the five students reviewed Sheri's rules for working in cooperative groups. They said:

- We cooperate with each other.
- We let everyone join in.
- We work it out. We compromise.

- We defer judgment. We don't laugh at others.
- We don't make negative comments.

● ● ● ● ● ● ● ● ● ● ● ● ● ● ● ●

How Are Concept Maps Constructed?

A concept map is a type of graphic organizer that includes a central idea with supporting facts or examples arranged from general to specific. To make a concept map, teachers and students can use the following steps, which are adapted from Ault, C. R. (1985) *Concept Mapping as a Study Strategy in Earth Sciences.*

1. Select major concept(s).
2. Brainstorm list of related words or ideas.
3. Organize items by clustering the words or ideas that are related.
4. Name each category.
5. Place the categories around the major concept.
6. Arrange the words that support each category.
7. Connect related categories with lines.
8. Label each line with words that describe the connection.

Remember, however, that these steps do not always occur in sequence; they are recursive. This means that at any time in the process, words and ideas can be reclustered or rearranged as students remember and rethink as they search for meaning.

• • • • • • • • • • • • • • •

Brainstorming and Categorizing

Sheri's students used their cooperative learning rules and Ault's eight steps, to create the concept map in Figure 3.1. They started with the heading "Grassland Animals" and brainstormed a list of words, writing them on the left side of a sheet of chart paper. Then they grouped words that went together and named each category of words. For example, Jill looked at the list and said, "Praying mantis and grasshopper are insects." She wrote *Insects* on the map with a green marker and added these two examples below the word. Each of the students used a different colored marker to identify other categories and the items within them. They wrote *Animals*

in pink, *Birds* in purple, and *Reptiles* in orange.

The students' conversation reconstructed here demonstrates how children use and develop their social skills as they create graphic organizers. Their discussions also convey how they engaged in shared meaning construction, elaboration, negotiation, and problem solving.

• • • • • • • • • • • • • • •

Shared Meaning Construction

When students share their individual knowledge, interact with one another, and hear other points of view, they build a common frame of understanding. The children in Sheri's class demonstrated shared meaning construction as they created the concept maps in Figures 3.1 and 3.2. Let's take a closer look at how they work together to create and revise their maps.

Sheri's students first called their map "Grassland Animals," but as they categorized and listed examples, they realized that several words (e.g., *corn*, *grass*, *wheat*, and *frog*) did not fit their original

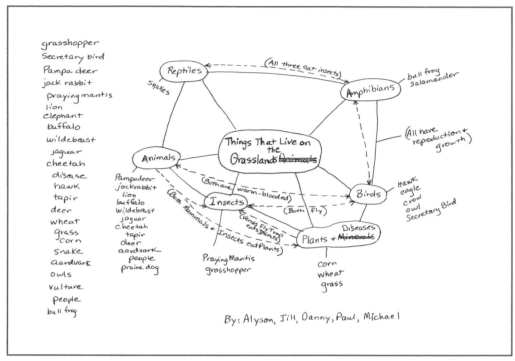

figure 3.1

figure 3.1   A concept map created by third grade students who worked in a cooperative group.

categories. Their dialogue demonstrates this:

Alyson: *"Corn* isn't an animal. And *grass* doesn't fit either."

Paul: "You're right. Neither does *wheat.* So, what do we do?"

Michael: "They're plants and we'd better add another circle."

Jill: "But, *plants* doesn't go with *Grassland Animals.*"

Alyson: "Why can't we change our title?"

Michael: "It can be 'Things That Live on the Grasslands!'"

The children agreed to change the title of their graphic organizer and create the new category, "Plants." Then Danny used a blue marker for the new category and wrote the words corn, grass, and wheat under it.

This discussion shows how questioning and active listening

helped the children discover a new category and rename their topic. By building a common frame of understanding, interacting with one another, and sharing individual knowledge, they problem-solved, negotiated, and constructed a new category, thus modifying their schema for grasslands.

Figure 3.2 shows the result of shared meaning construction, as well. It was created by three boys in the group who worked together to complete a partially designed concept map called "North China Plain." The map provided the boys with subtopics—"Industry," "Crops," "Climate," and "Changes in Farming." The boys reread sections of their textbook to identify examples for each category talked about together:

Paul: "The climate is cold and snowy there."

Dan: "I read in our social studies book that it is hot, and it's damp, too."

Michael: "Mrs. Serfass said there's lots of rain there!"

Dan: "It can't be cold and snowy and hot and damp at the same time. Can it?"

This thoughtful exchange led students into a meaningful discussion of seasons on the North China Plain. The children concluded that different seasons have different weather conditions. This conclusion was possible because they each shared a piece of specific knowledge and put the pieces together to create a better understanding of climate, seasons, and weather.

● ● ● ● ● ● ● ● ● ● ● ● ● ● ●

Elaboration

As students talk together about graphic organizers, they clarify and extend their understanding of content. In a word, they elaborate. For example, as the group created the map shown in Figure 3.1., Michael wanted to add *disease* to the brainstormed list, but the children questioned him and he explained his reasoning:

Danny: "What else can we add to the list?"

Michael: "Well, I know one that lives everywhere. It's not really an animal."

Danny: "What is it?"

Michael: *"Disease.* It's the only thing I can think of in

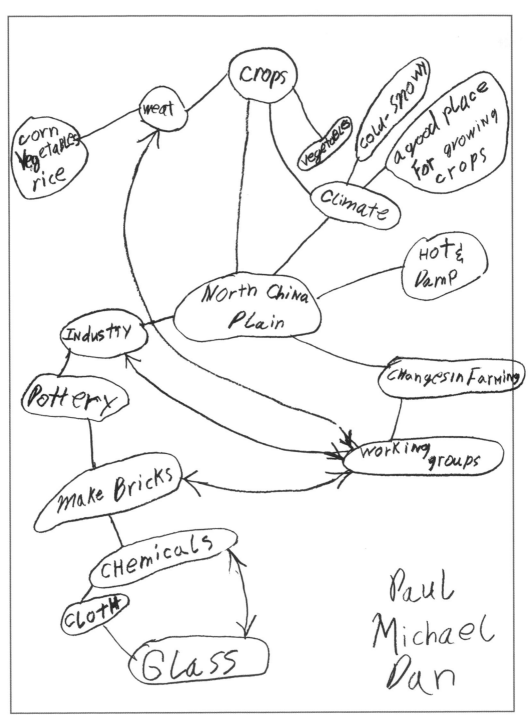

figure 3.2   Concept map using social studies content in a thematic study of grasslands.

my mind. 'Cause it's really sort of alive."

Paul: "Why? Do you think disease is an animal?"

Michael: "O.K. It's not an animal, but it's a living organism, and it's on the grasslands."

The group then decided it would be appropriate to add *disease* to the brainstorming list.

After the children wrote the categories and examples on the organizer, they were asked if they could see any connections among categories:

Danny: "How do you know they're both cold-blooded?"

Jill: "I think they are. But we'd better look it up."

Paul: "Animals and insects both eat plants."

Danny: "Insects and birds both fly."

Alyson: "Animals and birds are both warm-blooded."

Michael: "Reptiles and amphibians have reproduction and growth."

Danny: "What's reproduction?"

Michael: "They give birth to their young."

Jill: "You know, like all mothers have babies."

Then, the children began to see other relationships:

Michael: "Wait, I see a connection. Birds eat insects and plants. I'll draw a dotted line. Wait, I see another connection. Animals and birds are warm-blooded. I'll draw the dotted line."

Jill: "I see a connection. Both reptiles and amphibians are cold-blooded."

As these children made connections together among categories and examples, they exhibited higher levels of thinking and reasoning. They showed skills in synthesis and application as they talked, questioned, and made decisions about content. They also realized that when they did not have answers themselves, they needed to seek out answers in other resources.

Negotiation

Both during and after students construct meaning and elaborate their ideas, they have opportunities to use negotiation. Sheri's students, for example, compromised, mediated, and bargained among themselves until they reached consensus.

Negotiation occurred in the process of using colored markers to draw a final version of the organizer to share with the class. Jill had written "Amphibians" in green and when the group began to create the "Reptiles" category, the following negotiation took place:

Alyson: "Where's the green marker?"

Jill: "Don't use green for "Reptiles." They'll think that reptiles are amphibians."

Paul: "Hey, she's right. Reptiles aren't amphibians. Let's use a different color each time or they'll think we messed up."

figure 3.3　　A Venn diagram that compares and contrasts Kenya with North China.

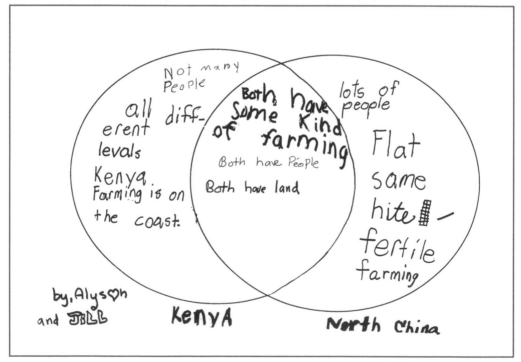

They continued to negotiate color choice as they discussed each category on the map. The group was aware of their audience and knew that their classmates could see the categories and differentiate among them more easily if each was in a different color.

Similarly, when Jill and Alyson paired up to complete a Venn diagram after reading a section of their text on Kenya and North China, (Figure 3.3.) they talked and negotiated as they filled in the diagram:

Jill: "The book says North China has fertile farming."

Alyson: "In Kenya farming is along the coast."

Jill: "In Kenya is there any farming on the plain?"

Alyson: "No, there's not enough moisture. It's a desert."

Jill: "So what should we put on the chart?"

Alyson: "Let's write 'both have land and both have farming.'"

Jill: "People live on the North China Plain and the Kenya Plain."

Alyson: "Wait a minute, it says only a few live on the Kenya Plain except near the coast."

Jill: "A few is still people."

Alyson: "So, let's just put that there are people in both."

Jill: "OK!"

During negotiation, it is evident that critical thinking and precise language play important roles. Children who focus on specific language and use it to express themselves are better able to reach consensus with peers through critical thinking, dialogue, and discussion.

● ● ● ● ● ● ● ● ● ● ● ● ● ●

Problem Solving

When students create concept maps, they also engage in finding solutions to problems that arise. This problem-solving skill, of course, enhances children's ability to understand literature. For example, one teacher read aloud *Bringing the Rain to Kapiti Plain* by Verna Aardema (Scholastic, 1981). She selected this Nandi folktale from Kenya

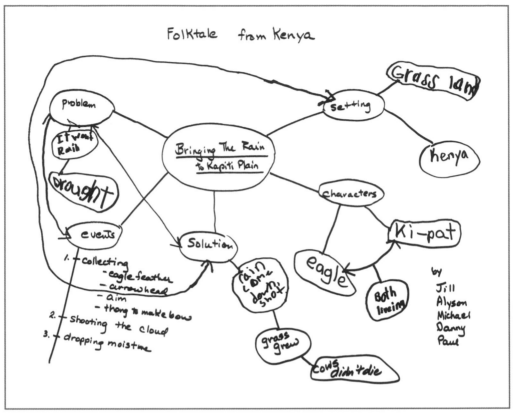

Folktale from Kenya

Grass land

problem

setting

It won't Rain

Bringing The Rain To Kapiti Plain

Kenya

Drought

Characters

events

Solution

Ki-pat

1. collecting
   - eagle feather
   - arrowhead
   - aim
   - thong to make bow
2. shooting the cloud
3. dropping moisture

rain come down shot

eagle

by
Jill
Alyson
Michael
Danny
Paul

Both living

grass grew

cows didn't die

figure 3.4   The story elements of a folktale *Bringing The Rain To Kapiti Plain* by V. Aardema, show the use of literature in social studies.

because it not only supports the social studies content, but contains a problem to be solved. Kipat, the main character, faced the problem of a terrible drought and had to solve it to save the plants and animals on the plain. Before she read the book aloud, the class was given a partially completed conceptual organizer containing the elements of a story—setting, characters, problem, events, and solution (see Figure 3.4). After an initial reading of the selection and a personal response by the class, the book was read again. This time the children were asked to form their cooperative groups for the purpose of completing the handout. Working together as a team, each group completed the task and supplied specific information before presenting their answers to the whole class.

The class discussion that followed these presentations centered on modern ways to solve a drought. The children came up with other solutions to solve the problem of drought, namely, "seeding the clouds," "ceremonial dances," and "prayer." These children were able to identify a problem and its solution not only in this story, but also were able to transfer this thinking to the real-life problem of drought today.

Another problem these students had was how to visually represent the connections they saw and share them with their classmates. When the list of words had been written on the map and the categories were determined, the students began to find connections:

Michael: "Everything is connected."

Paul: "So then, how can we show all these connections to them?"

Michael: "Use a different color."

Jill: "Use arrows."

Danny: "I've got it! We could uses dotted lines."

Michael: "We could use them all."

The group finally agreed to use dotted lines, color, and arrows to show how the various categories are connected. So, they negotiated and agreed the solution was to use aqua dotted lines with arrows pointing to the two connected categories. When the group reached consensus on how the categories were connected, they wrote the words in parentheses on the dotted lines and the problem was solved.

● ● ● ● ● ● ● ● ● ● ● ● ● ● ●

Benefits of Cooperatively Created Graphic Organizers

When teachers use cooperative learning and graphic organizers, students experience the benefits of both learning strategies. Several positive things occur:

• **Growth of social skills.** Students practice active listening, speaking, turn-taking, giving positive and constructive feedback, respecting one another, nurturing and supporting each other.

• **Development of strategic learning.** Students develop processes and strategies to actively construct meaning. They do this through brainstorming, categorizing, elaborating, negotiating, and problem solving as they grapple with content.

• **Improved questioning skills.** As students participate together to create graphic organizers, in all phases of the process they ask questions. They do this naturally in the context of the learning that is taking place.

• **Metacognitive ability.** Students who learn to use graphic organizers independently have a flexible strategy to use as they construct meaning. They can make choices among several types of graphic organizers depending on the structure of the task and its purpose.

• **Independent thinking.** Students who work cooperatively using graphic organizers are more easily able to produce graphic organizers on their own.

• **Higher levels of thinking and reasoning.** Students use analysis, synthesis, and evaluation in solving problems and thinking.

• **Positive attitudes toward learning.** Students develop more positive attitudes toward the subject and the experience of learning because of the social aspect of working cooperatively. They are motivated to learn about the subject and are more actively engaged in their own learning.

> **When teachers use cooperative learning and graphic organizers, students experience the benefits of both learning strategies.**

• **Increased respect for diversity and differences.** As students work in cooperative groups, they learn to value one another's diverse strengths, differences, abilities, styles, and needs.

• **Enhanced understanding and retention of content.** Students are better able to understand content and concepts. They have richer understandings and retain the information longer.

References

Ault, G. R. (1985). "Concept Mapping as a Study Strategy in Earth Sciences." *Journal of College Science Technology*, 15 (1), 38-44.

●●●●●●●●●●●●●●●●●●●●●●●●●●●●●●●●●●●

Further Reading

Kagan, S. (1992). *Cooperative Learning*. San Juan Capistrano, CA: Resources for Teachers.

Questions & Answers

Does cooperative grouping produce better graphic organizers?
　　Yes, in general, because the graphic organizer created by a cooperative group is the result of several students working together to pool and extend their knowledge, the end product is often better.

How do I use graphic organizers with students who do not know how to work collaboratively or cooperatively in a small group?
　　To institute cooperative grouping, it is best to organize your students into heterogeneous groups of four to five. Social skills such as active listening, turn-taking, respecting others, and giving constructive feedback can be taught or reviewed. One way to accomplish this is for you to model these behaviors and discuss each skill with your students. When they are familiar with key social skills, then you can use a "fishbowl" technique to refine the process: First, have a small group of children work together on the organizer while the rest of the class observes. Then the class can comment on and analyze what happened. Finally, the students can brainstorm ways to make the interaction more effective.

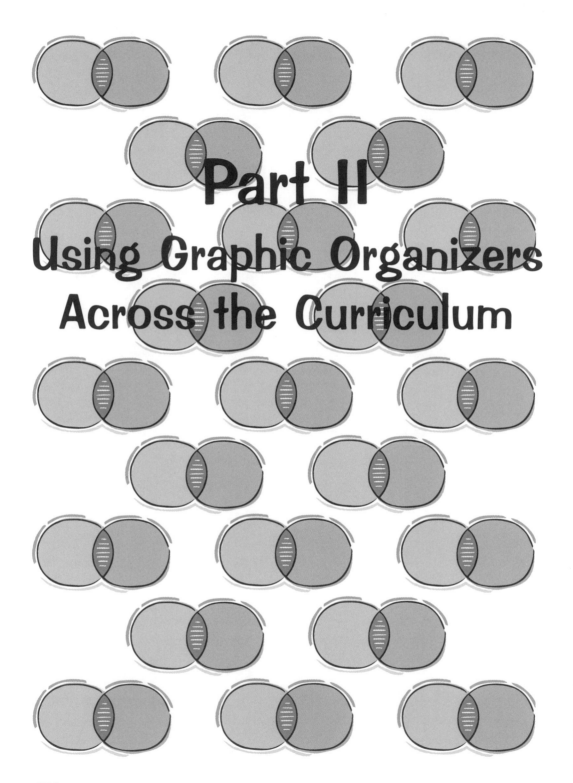

Part II
Using Graphic Organizers
Across the Curriculum

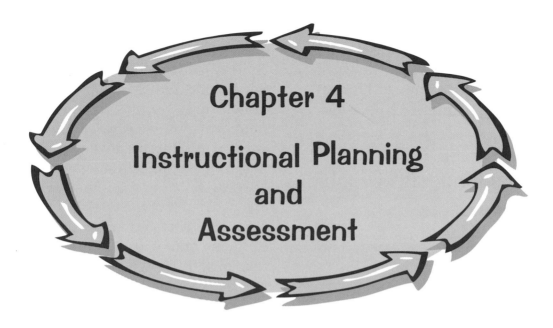

Chapter 4

Instructional Planning and Assessment

"It's hard for me to plan any other way now. A web is such an easy way to organize my thinking. I can put concepts, ideas, and infor-mation together and make connections that I never could see before." (Fourth grade teacher)

"As a testing tool the graphic organizer has possibilities I never considered, and my kids are excited about the option of creating these visual word pictures." (Eighth grade teacher)

These quotes from teachers who have recently begun using graphic organizers highlight some of the reasons teachers at all grade levels use them routinely to plan instruction and assess.

They give you a pictorial overview of the key elements in a unit of study and can be used as a tool to help you evaluate student learning—and your own teaching—at the end of a lesson or unit of study.

The graphic organizer is a way to determine an individual student's learning. When you ask students to create graphic organizers to show what they have learned, the organizers they construct will give you information to guide your future instruction. You will then know what to reteach or how to supplement with further instruction. The graphic organizer is sometimes used as an alternative to the more traditional essay or multiple-choice test format.

● ● ● ● ● ● ● ● ● ● ● ● ● ● ●

Planning with Graphic Organizers

Here are several advantages to using graphic organizers for instructional planning:
The graphic organizer is a flexible planning tool. Unlike an outline which is linear and sequential, the format of the graphic organizer allows for including ideas and information spontaneously, as they occur to you. For example, as you think about what you will teach and gather pertinent information, you can move back and forth recursively among the various categories on your graphic organizer to transcribe information and create a useful planning tool.

For an interdisciplinary unit on whales, Judith Reed, a second grade teacher, created a graphic organizer plan on a bulletin board (Figure 4.1) to guide the class's learning. Judith began with categories for ecology, literature, math, language arts, maps, and research. Later she added categories for introduction, art, and homework, added "magazines" to "Literature," and fleshed out other categories. After planning with a graphic organizer, Judith made a connection between "Research" and "Homework." She decided that the questions her students generated could be part of their homework. Notice the relationship shown with the dotted line that links "Homework" and "list ?'s for more info."

> **As you identify key concepts and include them on a graphic organizer, you isolate important information in a manner that often enbles you to see connections among topics that you might not otherwise notice.**

Using a graphic organizer for planning focuses your attention on key concepts. As you identify key concepts and include

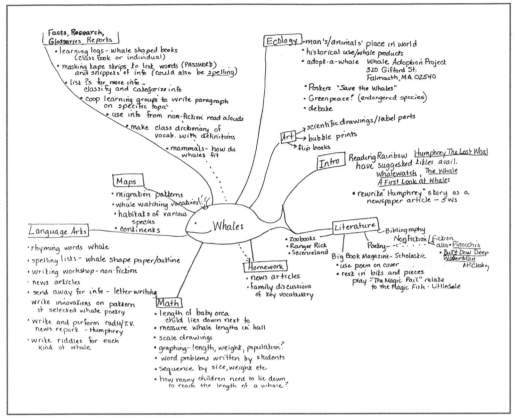

Facts, Research,
Glossaries Reports
• learning logs - whale shaped books
  (class book or individual)
• masking tape strips to list words (PASSWORD)
  and snippets of info (could also be *spelling*)
• list ?s for more info -
  classify and categorize info
• coop learning groups to write paragraph
  on specific topic
• use info from non-fiction read alouds
  • make class dictionary of
    vocab. with definitions
  • mammals - how do
    whales fit

Ecology - man's/animals' place in world
  • historical use/whale products
  • adopt-a-whale Whale Adoption Project
                   320 Gifford St.
                   Falmouth, MA 02540
  • Posters "Save the Whales"
  • Greenpeace! (endangered species)
  • debate

Art → scientific drawings/label parts
    → bubble prints
    → flip books

Intro Reading Rainbow Humphrey The Lost Whale
       have suggested titles avail.
       Whalewatch , The Whale
       A First Look at Whales
  • rewrite "Humphrey" story as a
    newspaper article - 5 Ws

Maps
• migration patterns
• whale watching vocations
• habitats of various
  species
• continents

Language Arts
• rhyming words whale
• spelling lists - whale shape paper/outline
• writing workshop - non-fiction
• news articles
• send away for info - letter writing
  write innovations on pattern
  of selected whale poetry
• write and perform radio/T.V.
  news report - Humphrey
• write riddles for each
  kind of whale

Whales

Literature — Bibliography
  Non Fiction — Fiction
  Poetry - .... also - Pinocchio
  Big Book Magazine - Scholastic • But Dow Deep
  • use poem on cover   WaterMan
  • rest in bits and pieces   McCloskey
    play "The Magic Pail" relate
    to the Magic Fish - Littledale
• Zoobooks
• Ranger Rick
• Scienceland

Homework
• news articles
• family discussions
  of key vocabulary

Math
• length of baby orca
  child lies down next to
• measure whale lengths in hall
• scale drawings
• graphing - length, weight, population?
• word problems written by students
• sequence by size, weight etc.
• how many children need to lie down
  to reach the length of a whale?

figure 4.1   Judith Reed's integrated unit plan on a study of whales.

them on a graphic organizer, you isolate important information in a manner that often enbles you to see connections among topics that you might not otherwise notice. If your planning includes using a content area text, creating a graphic organizer helps you illustrate this content and become aware of how well the text is organized. You notice what information or concepts may have been omitted and what other supplementary materials you should include. Graphic organizers may also make it easier to match mandated curriculum with key concepts from the text; with the text's important information isolated on the organizer, you can tell at a glance whether the two match and what you may have omitted.

Since the format of the graphic organizer is flexible and less constraining than the typical linear outline, it is also useful when you brainstorm a plan with a group of students. For example, when a sixth grade teacher talked with her students in September to identify the different kinds of books they could read during the year, she used a graphic organizer. She provided them with two key concepts—"fiction" and "nonfiction"—and the definitions "true fact" and "not true-made up." As the students talked about books they had read recently, they identified different types of books such as science fiction, autobiography, sports, mystery, adventure, science, history, and romance. The teacher added these genres to the organizer.

The graphic organizer is especially appropriate for thematic and interdisciplinary instruction. If you are moving toward thematic instruction as a way of teaching, the graphic organizer is a valuable tool, as it lends itself to the creation of interdisciplinary units. The pictorial overview of a unit that a graphic organizer provides makes it easy to see connections with other subjects. At a glance, you have the "whole picture" of what you will teach, and you can make associations more easily than you might with a typical outline plan, as Judith did with her graphic organizer on whales.

Students can also use them as a planning tool for their own thematic or interdisciplinary projects. Teachers who use inquiry-oriented instruction often have students create their own plans for their individual inquiry and research. Many teachers encourage their students to use the same "web" format Judith used (Figure 4.1) to direct their research. First, have each of your students create several major categories related to his or her topic. Next, have students add ideas as they occur, moving back and forth among categories. Then, your students can generate questions they hope to answer with their research and data collection and a list of possible resources they will use.

• • • • • • • • • • • • • • • •

An Assessment Ally

Again, graphic organizers are powerful assessment tools. Here's why:

Key concepts from a graphic organizer form the basis for assessment and evaluation of teaching. If the graphic organizer represents what you taught during a unit, then it can guide your decisions about what to test at the end of the unit. You can create

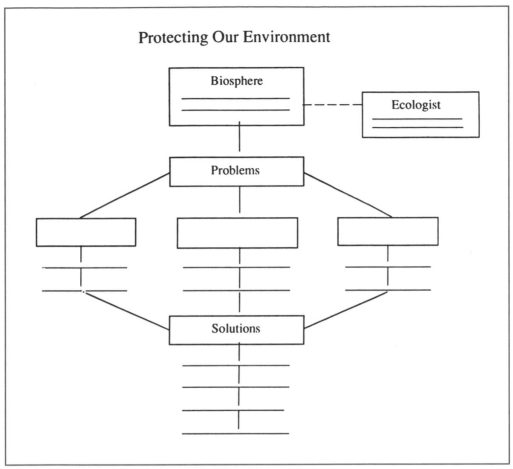

figure 4.2   A teacher-created hierarchical organizer on the biosphere to which students can add examples and information showing what they have learned.

your test directly from the key concepts and main ideas included on the graphic organizer you used for planning. In this way, you form a closer link between instruction and assessment and are less apt to test only part of what you taught or test what you did not teach at all. After assessing student learning, you can use this information to plan your future instruction; you will know what your students have learned well and what they still need to know.

You can even use the key categories on your instructional organizer to create essay questions that link various concepts. In so doing, you are more apt to foster critical and creative thinking and measure the broad knowledge and understandings your stu-

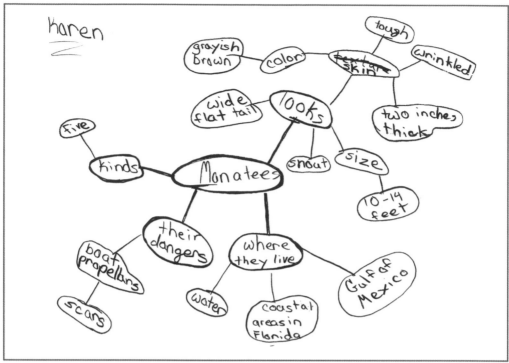

figure 4.3   Karen shows what she has learned about manatees by making her own graphic organizer.

dents possess. For example, Judith could ask her students a question that links "Maps" and "Ecology," such as "Which types of whales are endangered and how have their migration patterns contributed to their decline?"

The graphic organizer is an option for measuring student learning. Some teachers give students the option of creating a graphic organizer to show what they have learned, in place of, or along with, other ways of assessing learning. However, your students need to have a solid under-standing of the graphic organizer strategy before you expect them to use it as a way of demonstrating knowledge and understanding of a topic.

Here are some ideas for using graphic organizers to assess student learning:

1. Furnish all key words and ask your students to generate a graphic organizer that depicts relationships among those words.

2. Provide key words for the major categories and ask your stu-

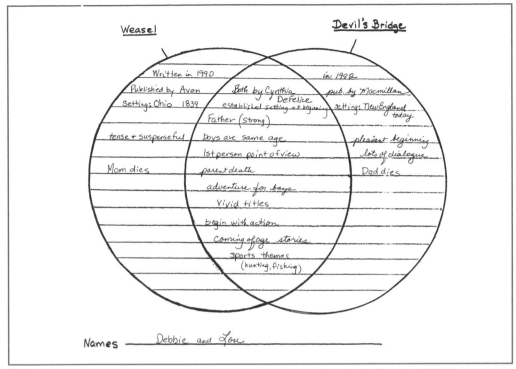

figure 4.4 Two students created a Venn diagram on books by Cynthia DeFelice.

dents to supply information and examples that represent these categories. See Figure 4.2 for an example of a teacher-created hierarchical organizer for the social studies concept "biosphere."

3. Furnish a blank organizer that shows categories and relationships without key words and ask students to supply this vocabulary.

4. Encourage students to use a graphic organizer you provide as a prewriting strategy for an essay question.

5. Allow students to create their own organizer by identifying key words themselves and selecting the format that best fits the content. See Figure 4.3 for an example of a concept organizer created by a fourth grader.

6. Use these ideas not only with individual students, but also with small cooperative groups. See Figure 4.4 for an example of a Venn diagram created by two students who each read a different book by Cynthia DeFelice, *Weasel* (Avon, 1990)

and *Devil's Bridge* (Macmillan, 1992).

7. Ultimately, you can ask students who are proficient in the construction of graphic organizers to demonstrate their understanding of information by having them generate original organizers. Of course, a student-created graphic organizer is most effective as an assessment tool when the student explains it to you orally or writes a brief explanation.

For example, in her verbal explanation of the "Manatees" web (Figure 4.3) fourth grader Karen identified information and relationships orally that she did not include on the organizer. In rereading her web she realized that "color," "tough," "wrinkled," and "two inches thick" did not fit under "texture," so she changed the category to "Skin." In discussion, she articulated that sharks and alligators could be enemies of manatees. She also said she could add "weight" and "1200 to 1500 pounds" to "Looks," and she created a new category, "Relatives," with "dugany" as an example.

Creating a graphic organizer to represent knowledge allows your students to identify important concepts and supporting information quickly, as well as represent the relationships among them. It is not as constraining as the written essay since students do not need to compose the longer expository text of an essay. The graphic organizer often provides more information about what a student has learned than a multiple-choice question since the student can show linkages and supporting information in a graphic organizer that he or she could not show in a multiple-choice response.

The graphic organizer is one way to reflect and confer about student strengths and needs. Since a conceptual organizer allows you to see many different kinds of related information at a glance, it is a good way to begin a discussion of student progress when conferring with parents and others. Graphic organizer like the one in Figure 4.5 (on page 53) give parents, the student, another teacher, or an administrator a balanced view of the student's strengths and needs.

Using this organizer, James's teacher was easily able to discuss his developing behaviors and needs in the context of his strengths. James might also reflect on his own learning in a graphic-organizer format.

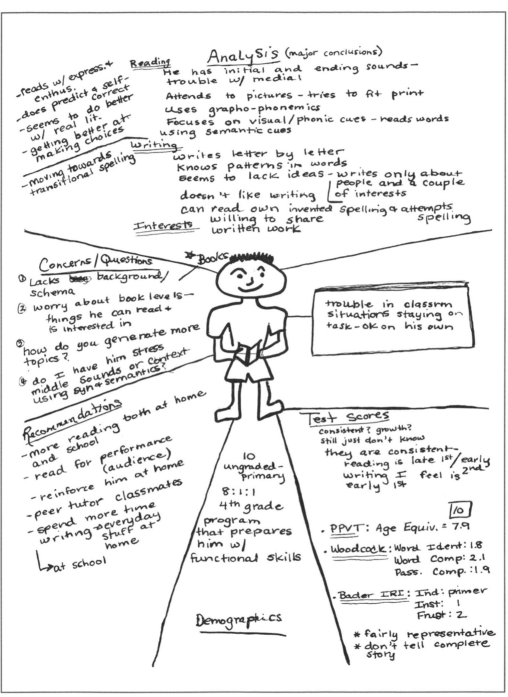

Analysis (major conclusions)

Reading

He has initial and ending sounds – trouble w/ medial

Attends to pictures – tries to fit print

Uses grapho-phonemics

Focuses on visual/phonic cues – reads words using semantic cues

-reads w/ express.+ enthus.
-does predict & self-correct
-seems to do better w/ real lit.
-getting better at making choices
-moving towards transitional spelling

Writing

Writes letter by letter

Knows patterns in words

Seems to lack ideas – writes only about people and a couple of interests

doesn't like writing

can read own invented spelling & attempts spelling

willing to share written work

Interests

* Books

Concerns / Questions

① Lacks background/schema

② worry about book levels – things he can read + is interested in

③ how do you generate more topics?

④ do I have him stress middle sounds or context using syn & semantics?

trouble in classrm situations staying on task – ok on his own

Recommendations

-more reading both at home and school

- read for performance (audience)

- reinforce him at home

-peer tutor classmates

- spend more time writing everyday stuff at home

↳ at school

10 ungraded-primary

8:1:1

4th grade program that prepares him w/ functional skills

Demographics

Test Scores

consistent? growth?
still just don't know
they are consistent-
reading is late 1st/early
writing I feel is 2nd
early 1st

10

• PPVT: Age Equiv. = 7.9

• Woodcock: Word Ident: 1.8
Word Comp: 2.1
Pass. Comp.: 1.9

• Bader IRI: Ind: primer
Inst: 1
Frust: 2

* fairly representative
* don't tell complete story

figure 4.5   A teacher-created graphic organizer for conferring about James's strengths and developing behaviors.

It is much easier for parents to see success in one area, balanced by developing behaviors or understandings in other areas, when the whole student is represented in this way. This type of organizer provides a positive way to discuss a student's progress. You can add new areas of learning to the organizer and check off goals that have been accomplished as the student acquires new knowledge and skills.

You will undoubtedly adapt the ideas in this chapter to your own needs and find other creative ways to use graphic organizers to help you become a more effective teacher.

● ●

Further Reading

Bromley, K. (1992). *Webbing with Literature*. Boston: Allyn & Bacon.

Norton, D.E. (1992). *The Impact of Literature-Based Reading*. New York: Macmillan.

Rafferty, C.D. (1993). "Concept Mapping: A Viable Alternative to Objective and Essay Exams." Reading Research and Instruction, 32 (3), 25-34.

Questions & Answers

How do I deal with evaluation and grades related to graphic organizers?

It is your option to grade or not to grade graphic organizers. We recommend a holistic evaluation of graphic organizers that includes credit for key concepts, supporting information, and connections among these ideas, as well. Graphic organizers can be an alternative or optional way for students to demonstrate knowledge and learning, however. Often, students who become proficient with graphic organizers use them in place of traditional essay responses on tests.

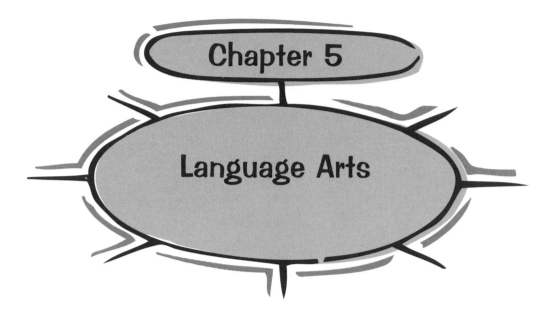

Chapter 5

Language Arts

Patricia Ciotoli, a fifth grade teacher, creates a web to help her focus on her purposes for using literature in the classroom. "It reminds me to use the power of literature for language literacy, curriculum connections, for learning about life, and most of all for the pure pleasure of it!" she says.

Pat uses a web (Figure 5.1) as a planning tool, as well as a vision for the role of literature in her program. She regularly shares it with the students in her class and, over time, she and the students add details to the web, such as "USSR," "man vs. nature," "writing process," and "immigration." School weeks go by. This web highlights for Pat and her students that literature:

1. Brings joy to their lives and helps them solve problems
2. Develops language skills in a natural way
3. Makes history come alive
4. Increases their understanding of people, society, and the environment
5. Enhances and expands their schemata of human existence through such themes as friendship, change, and aging.

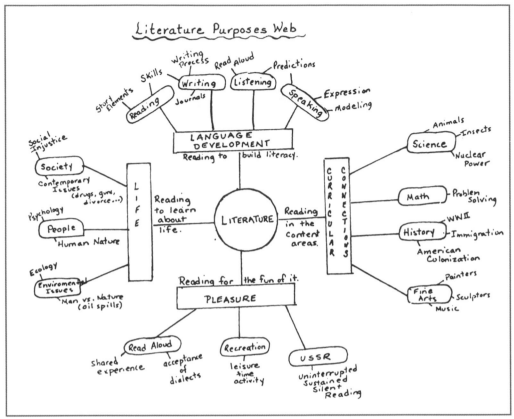

figure 5.1   A fifth grade teacher's planning web emphasizes the many purposes of literature-based instruction.

This chapter will attempt to demonstrate some of the varied uses that graphic organizers play in Pat's and other teachers' language arts classrooms.

These organizers are examples of the ways that visual representations can assist students. They are helpful in prereading, during reading, postreading, in media other than print, and in the stages of the writing process.

Prereading

Many teachers use graphic organizers to prepare their students for reading or listening. Teachers assess students' prior knowledge and experiential background and represent this knowledge visually for students. Teachers often have students brainstorm, clarify, categorize, and prioritize the knowledge they have about a question or concept.

This builds a common knowledge base and motivates students to read the selection.

During brainstorming, students often use vocabulary they will encounter when they read the story. You can also add preselected vocabulary that you feel is necessary for students to be able to read and understand. In this way you can use graphic organizers for vocabulary development before reading.

> **Many teachers use graphic organizers to prepare their students for reading or listening. Teachers assess students' prior knowledge and experiential background and represent this knowledge visually for students.**

Some teachers prepare organizers to use before reading to set the scene or introduce a story. For example, you might share a graphic organizer with the characters, setting, and the problem for a particular book. Discussion of these story elements gives students an overview and preparation for reading so they can make connections between what they read or hear and the information that was introduced on the organizer.

● ● ● ● ● ● ● ● ● ● ● ● ● ● ●

During Reading

One strategy taught to students for structuring and representing knowledge that is commonly a part of language arts classes is that of sequencing. Sequencing requires students to put the events of a story or selection they're reading in the order in which the events occur. A sequence can contain a specific beginning and end (chronology) or can be cyclical if it shows a series of events in a circular formation.

Working with at-risk students from second grade, Jan Kemmery, a reading specialist who works with Chapter I students, decided to use a cyclical organizer in literature. She read aloud *If You Give a Mouse a Cookie* by Laura Numeroff (HarperCollins, 1985). She asked

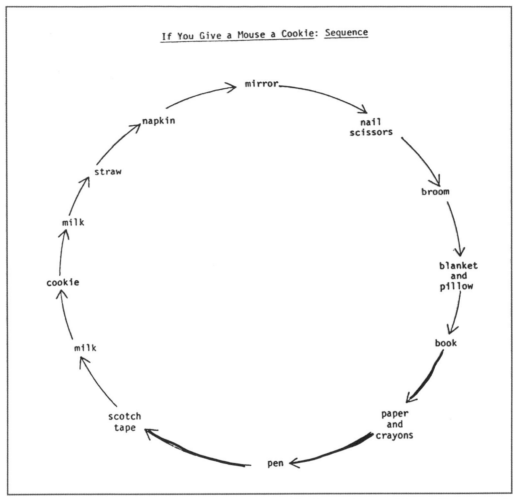

figure 5.2   Reading teacher Jan Kemmery's cyclical organizer models retelling a story in sequence.

the children to respond personally to the story first, and then led a discussion of the events that occurred and the order in which they happened. She drew Figure 5.2 while the children retold the story in sequence.

As the organizer conveys, the class was delighted to see that the story could just go "on and on forever."

Jan's next opportunity to use a graphic organizer with this group came when the children read *Curious George Rides a Bike* by H. A. Ray (Houghton Mifflin, 1952). Again, Jan used several reading strategies with the story.

For a culminating activity, she invited the children to list the cycle of events as they occurred in sequence. The class had a lively discussion about "what happened next" and were encouraged to go back to the story to verify their responses. Fortunately, this story is full of interesting events that children delight in recounting.

They reached consensus about the episodes and then wrote summary statements and illustrations to match (Figure 5.3). The children then suggested to Jan that she number the events and put them in a circle "the same way we did with the mouse and cookie book" which Jan promptly did.

Matthew, Kris, and Andrew were pleased to use this visual (reproduced below) when retelling the story to other classmates as well as the school principal.

They proudly showed their graphic organizer as they practiced oral speaking skills.

figure 5.3   Children create this cyclical organizer after reading *Curious George Ride a Bike*.

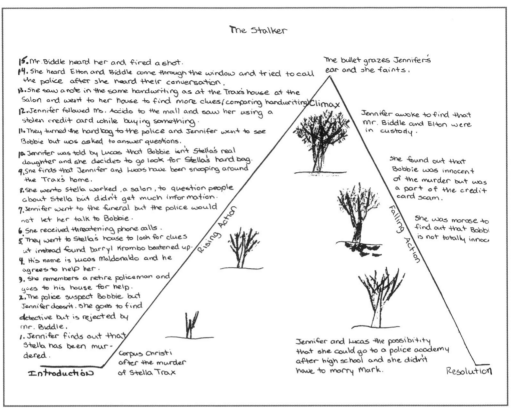

The Stalker

15. Mr. Biddle heard her and fired a shot.

14. She heard Elton and Biddle come through the window and tried to call the police after she heard their conversation.

13. She saw a note in the same handwriting as at the Trax's house at the Salon and went to her house to find more clues (comparing handwriting). Climax

12. Jennifer followed Ms. Acido to the mall and saw her using a stolen credit card while buying something.

11. They turned the hand bag to the police and Jennifer went to see Bobbie but was asked to answer questions.

10. Jennifer was told by Lucas that Bobbie isn't Stella's real daughter and she decides to go look for Stella's hand bag.

9. She finds that Jennifer and Lucas have been snooping around the Trax's home.

8. She went to Stella worked, a salon, to question people about Stella but didn't get much information.

7. Jennifer went to the funeral but the police would not let her talk to Bobbie.

6. She received threatening phone calls.

5. They went to Stella's house to look for clues it instead found Darryl Krambo beaten up.

4. His name is Lucas Maldonaldo and he agrees to help her.

3. She remembers a retire policeman and goes to his house for help.

2. The police suspect Bobbie but Jennifer doesn't. She goes to find detective but is rejected by Mr. Biddle.

1. Jennifer finds out that Stella has been murdered.

Rising Action

Introduction

Corpus Christi after the murder of Stella Trax

The bullet grazes Jennifer's ear and she faints.

Jennifer awoke to find that Mr. Biddle and Elton were in custody.

She found out that Bobbie was innocent of the murder but was a part of the credit card scam.

She was morose to find out that Bobbi is not totally innoc.

Falling Action

Jennifer and Lucas the possibility that she could go to a police academy after high school and she didn't have to marry Mark.

Resolution

figure 5.4   Eighth grader Lan's plot diagram reflects her summary of the events in *The Stalker* by Joan Lowery Nixon.

Postreading

Kathy Buckner, a reading teacher in a middle school, offers yet another look at graphic organizers, but in a postreading setting. Kathy's eighth grade reading class consists of gifted students whose assignment is to depict a piece of literature of their choosing in a visual way. Kathy, who learned of graphic organizers when she took a content area reading course for her Master's Degree in Reading, has taught the students to use a variety of graphic organizers in her literature-based/whole language classroom. First, Kathy modeled the organizer—which she calls a plot diagram—with the book *The Princess Bride*, by William Goldman (Ballantine, 1987) because it is a favorite of the students. Now the students know how to use the organizer to illustrate the plot of any novel they are reading. Kathy has also worked with the youngsters on writing brief summary statements throughout the school year, a skill which she believes is integral to producing plot organizers.

Thus, two students selecting the same novel can use the plot diagram in different ways to depict their understanding and comprehension of the events of a story. They can use their individual creativity to design symbols that have meaning to them.

Lan, an eighth grader, chose to use an organizer (Figure 5.4, on page 60) to show the important parts of a book she'd just completed, *The Stalker* by Joan Lowery Nixon (Delacorte, 1985). Lan summarizes the episodes by writing sentences that describe the introduction and the rising action that leads to the climax of the story.

Next, Lan traces the falling action after the climax until the story has a resolution, or denouement. The illustrations Lan creates center on the symbol of the tree as it emerges, grows, and sprouts foliage until (at the climax), it is in full bloom. To represent the falling action, Lan depicts a tree's leaves changing color and falling off until (at the resolution), the tree is dormant and completely bare. The cycle of the tree's development is Lan's way of describing the terms in the plot diagram.

Eighth grader Linda creates another illustration for the same novel (Figure 5.5). She sees the plot diagram as a "Suspense-0-Meter: Heat Rating" for this exciting book. Linda portrays the introduction as the spark ("suspense barely started") through the rising action, where the flame is lit, to the high point of suspense where the climax is pictured as a fire. For the falling action, Linda draws a bucket of water that cools down the story until the fire is out (resolution or end).

● ● ● ● ● ● ● ● ● ● ● ● ● ● ● ● ●

Beyond Print

Knowledge from sources other than print can be represented with graphic organizers as well. The example in Figure 5.6 shows how third grade students compared the book and video of *Stone Fox* by John Reynolds Gardiner (HarperCollins, 1983). Reading specialist Jan Kemmery and third grade teacher Gerry Tastle used Venn diagrams to design the book-video comparison, doing lots of preplanning to insure congruence between Jan's pull-out program and Gerry's

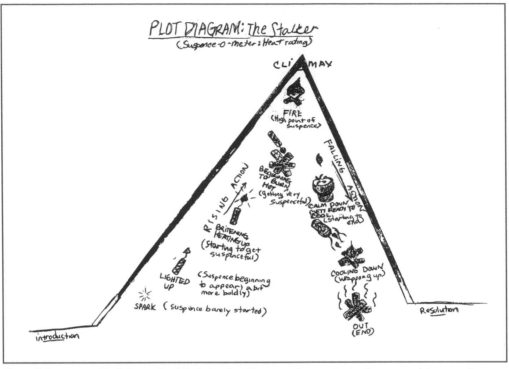

PLOT DIAGRAM: The Stalker
(Suspence-o-meter: Heat rating)

CLIMAX

FIRE
(High point of suspence)

RISING ACTION

FALLING ACTION

BEGINNING TO BURN HOT
(getting very suspenceful)

CALM DOWN, GETTING COOL
(starting to end)

BRITENING HEATING UP
(Starting to get suspenceful)

COOLING DOWN
(wrapping up)

LIGHTED UP

(Suspence beginning to appear) a bit more boldly)

SPARK (suspence barely started)

Resolution

OUT
(END)

introduction

figure 5.5   Eighth grader Linda's plot diagram demonstrates how graphic organizers invite student creativity and individuality.

language arts curriculum. (Gerry's class had 24 students, including five Chapter I students.)

For several weeks Jan assisted the Chapter I students as they read *Stone Fox*. She pretaught vocabulary, combined oral and silent reading strategies, and checked for comprehension. Children kept journals and responded to the story based on their own experiential backgrounds. The other students in Gerry's class read *Stone Fox* independently with some guidance from Gerry.

After the children finished the story, they viewed a video in Gerry's classroom over the course of several days. The teachers worked as a team to motivate students to view the movie, telling them there were some surprising differences between the video and the book. When the video ended, the class spontaneously declared "We liked the book better!" This was the perfect "teachable moment," and Gerry and Jan immediately invited the students to brainstorm the likenesses and differences between the book and the movie. Figure 5.6 illustrates some of the comparisons the class made, although the actual list from that day contained nearly 85 entries!

Then the class moved from the Venn diagram to a more focused comparison between the movie and the book. The children formed cooperative groups of four and each group prepared a graphic organizer like the one in Figure 5.7. First, they decided on broad categories, or characteristics, such as setting, plot, characters, and descriptions. Then, after discussing how the movie dealt with each characteristic, they wrote a statement about each on a line extending from the right side of the category.

They discussed how the book portrayed the same characteristic, and wrote that statement on the left side of the category. A reader could easily understand the differences between the two media.

figure 5.6   A third grade class's Venn diagram comparing the video *Stone Fox* with the book *Stone Fox* by John Reynolds Gardiner.

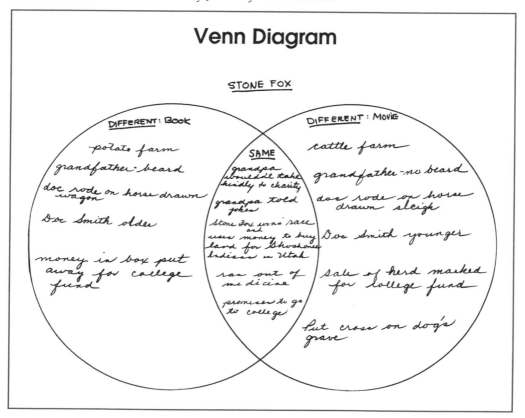

Venn Diagram

STONE FOX

DIFFERENT: BOOK

potato farm
grandfather: beard
doc rode on horse drawn wagon
Doc Smith older
money in box put away for college fund

SAME

grandpa and should/will take kindly to charity
grandpa told jokes
Stone Fox wins race uses money to buy land for Shoshone Indians in Utah
ran out of medicine
promises to go to college

DIFFERENT: MOVIE

cattle farm
grandfather - no beard
doc rode on horse drawn sleigh
Doc Smith younger
sale of herd marked for college fund
put cross on dog's grave

Stone Fox

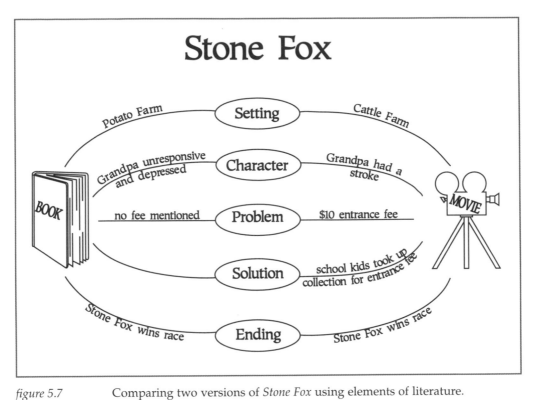

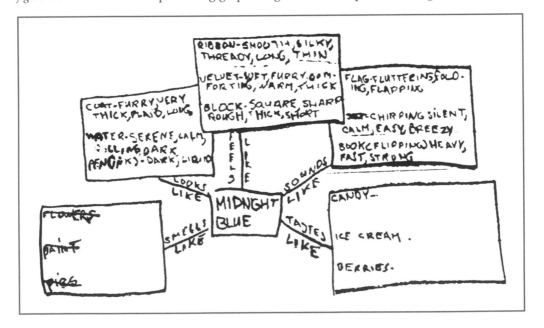

figure 5.7   Comparing two versions of *Stone Fox* using elements of literature.

figure 5.8   Blaine's prewriting graphic organizer for his poem "Midnight Blue."

Writing

During a poetry unit, Pat Ciotoli instructed her students to organize their thoughts prior to writing the first draft of a poem. In figure 5.8, Blaine incorporates the five senses to produce a series of ideas for his poem entitled "Midnight Blue," using these categories: "smells like," "looks like," "feels like," "sounds like," and "tastes like." Key words, such as *ribbon*, *velvet*, or *water*, remind him of his title "Midnight Blue." He uses descriptive words to further describe the key word, such as *serene* for water, and *silky* for ribbon. You can see from Blaine's organizer that prior to writing his poem, he makes decisions about what to keep and what to reject. His visual representation makes it easier to keep a record of his thoughts, ideas, and vocabulary as he begins to write. Blaine actually played with phrases such as "smells like flowers coated with dew," which eventually became the first line of his final draft:

Midnight Blue

Midnight Blue smells like flowers coated with dew
  And who would doubt that, who, who, who?
 It also smells like wet paint on the wall
  And the pie that beats them all.

This color sounds like crickets in the night;
  Which, I can say can give me a fright
 It's also our fluttering, flying flag
  And the sky next to the great white stag;
 It's my really exciting book:
  Which has some very good looks.

It looks like a warm winter coat
  And the water in a castle moat.
 It is the pen with which I write,
  It also is my flying kite.

It tastes like a cool, sweet berry
  Which, I say, makes me merry.
 It is blueberry ice cream
  Which is sweet; it always seems.
 Midnight Blue is my good candy
  Which makes me dandy.

Finally, Midnight Blue is my sister's felt,
  Next to her favorite belt.
 It is her velvet so soft,
  Which I feel merrily in the loft;
 It is my building block
  Which, of course, is like a rock.

Midnight Blue makes me feel so eternally
  Which I feel all of internally.
 Midnight Blue is beautifully calm,
  Which I admire while in the palm.
 Midnight Blue is the calm, starry sky
  Which makes me so tired, why would I lie?

Midnight Blue is beautiful.

By Blaine

Pat has incorporated peer-conferencing into her writing workshop. In one instance, students worked in a collaborative setting with Blaine and used a revising checklist. This gives Blaine feedback on areas needing improvement, such as "more descriptive," "more detailed," and "more interesting." Blaine accepts classmates' feedback and proceeds to incorporate their suggestions into his final poem. Pat has added a unique feature to her writing workshop: She sends the final checklist home to allow parents to provide more assistance in spelling, punctuating, and paragraphing. The parent signs and returns it to Pat via their child.

● ● ● ● ● ● ● ● ● ● ● ● ● ● ●

Conclusion

Graphic organizers benefit literacy learning by:

1. Improving comprehension skills and strategies
2. Facilitating the recalling or retelling of literature
3. Connecting prior knowledge and new knowledge for students
4. Easing the organization and direction of student writing.

In this chapter we have provided models from several elementary classrooms to show graphic organizers' flexibility in language arts:

• **Prereading**. For assessing and sharing prior knowledge, vocabulary development, and setting the scene.

• **During reading**. For setting a purpose, focusing student attention on specific information, or developing concepts.

• **Postreading.** To retell or recall what has been read, as an outline for writing process activities, and as a study guide for later review.

• **Writing.** To plan and organize thoughts before writing and to guide writing.

• **Comparing print and nonprint.** Contrasting story components from literature with similar components in movies, video, and audio tapes.

Many K-8 teachers have learned to use graphic organizers in a variety of ways to build their students' language arts abilities, developing effective listening, speaking, reading, and writing skills.

Further Reading

Curran, Lorna. (1992). *Cooperative Learning Lessons for Little Ones: Literature Based Language Arts and Social Skills.* San Juan Capistrano, CA: Resources for Teachers, Inc.

Stone, Jeanne M. (1991). *Cooperative Learning and Language Arts.* San Juan Capistrano, CA: Resources for Teachers, Inc.

Questions & Answers

Is it all right to ask my students occassionally to create a graphic organizer in their journals in place of writing narrative?

Absolutely! The graphic organizer is an appropriate format for entries in journals, learning logs, or as part of class notes. Varying the format of journal entries can heighten student interest and stimulate "tired" journals. In fact, students who are proficient with graphic organizers frequently choose them as the most appropriate means of recording information.

Do graphic organizers decrease or eliminate the need for students to write?

No. While graphic organizers sometimes replace an essay, there must still be many opportunities for students to write expository pieces and develop written fluency. The graphic organizer can, however, serve as a prewriting strategy for an essay and can replace the typical linear outline commonly used at this early stage of writing.

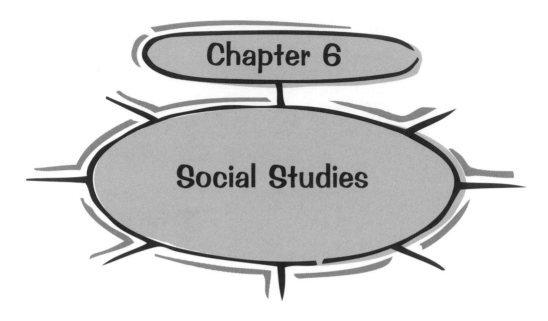

Chapter 6

Social Studies

"History is boring. It's just memorizing names and dates," declared Garrett, a high school senior, in response to a question about his history courses. When asked why he felt this way, Garrett described his experiences in social studies classes by saying, among other things, "We always read a chapter and answer the questions at the end." Like Garrett, many students view social studies and history as a collection of irrelevant, unrelated dates and facts. It seems that some teachers pay little attention to concepts and relationships that make history come alive for their students.

Currently, in many states, a change is taking place that will please students like Garrett. In the new model, curriculum is now defined as more then just a series of facts organized according to subject matter.

In New York State, for example, the relationship and balance among skills, content, and concepts is an important part of the new paradigm for instruction in the social studies (see Figure 6.1).

The essential skills and dispositions which will guide future social studies instruction by educators include:

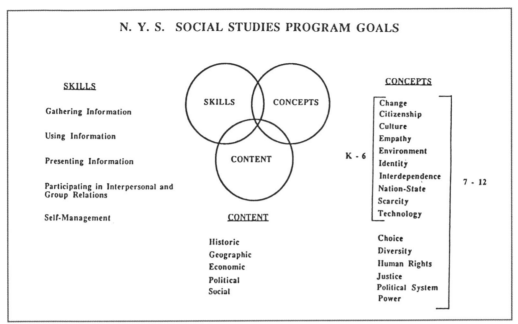

N. Y. S. SOCIAL STUDIES PROGRAM GOALS

SKILLS

Gathering Information

Using Information

Presenting Information

Participating in Interpersonal and
Group Relations

Self-Management

CONTENT

Historic
Geographic
Economic
Political
Social

CONCEPTS

Change
Citizenship
Culture
Empathy
Environment
Identity
Interdependence
Nation-State
Scarcity
Technology

Choice
Diversity
Human Rights
Justice
Political System
Power

K - 6

7 - 12

figure 6.1   New York State's framework for Social studies on which each theme unit, and lesson should be based.

- Managing Resources
- Managing Information
- Developing Personal Qualities and Dispositions
- Developing Interpersonal and Citizenship Competencies
- Working with Systems and Technology
- Developing Entrepreneurial Skills
- Thinking, Solving Problems, Creating

Teachers who use the new curriculum framework are focus-ing on concepts such as environment, justice, and diversity by teaching such skills as gathering, using, and presenting information as they teach the content of economics, geography, and history. These strands have application at all grade levels. Just as the State Education Department has used a graphic organizer to depict their view of social studies curriculum in New York State, many teachers are using graphic organizers to show relationships among concepts, to liven up their social studies programs, and make learning more meaningful for students. However, graphic organizers can have benefits beyond these. They can help develop students who will be able to work productively and participate effectively in a democratic society. When students work with graphic organizers in a cooperative learning setting, they use skills and strategies that eventually transfer to the workplace and society. In becoming adept at using graphic organizers, students gain the ability to analyze and evaluate information from a wide spectrum of sources, including print, film, lecture, and video. In the social studies, graphic organizers can depict common patterns of knowledge organization in social studies, which are:

• **Sequential.** Events arranged in chronological order.

• **Conceptual.** A central idea with supporting facts surrounding it.

• **Hierarchical.** A main concept with subconcepts under it.

● ● ● ● ● ● ● ● ● ● ● ● ● ● ● ●

A Sequential Organizer

Any thinking or problem-solving situation includes drawing upon essential skills and expressing one's creativity through different types of intelligence. One such type of intelligence is logical, or sequential, intelligence. Pat Ciotoli develops in her fifth grade social studies class through the use of time lines, a commonly used graphic organizer. Pat has her students keep a time line throughout the school year so that they can put historical events in perspective. The time line helps students make connections and understand complex relationships and interrelationships. Creating them helps students view events in history from multiple perspectives and allows them to synthesize and evaluate new knowledge in new situations. Comparing and contrasting, drawing inferences, hypothesizing, and predicting—these are some of the essential skills and dispositions that students have when creating a time line.

In Figure 6.2, we see a part of a time line created by Emily, a student in Pat's class, who attempts to depict the 1950's through the 1990's by writing what she feels are critical years: 1955, 1957, 1960, and so on. Emily decides not to include every year along the continuum, but only those which have meaning for her. Emily also divides her time line into two categories, which she labels "foreign connection" and

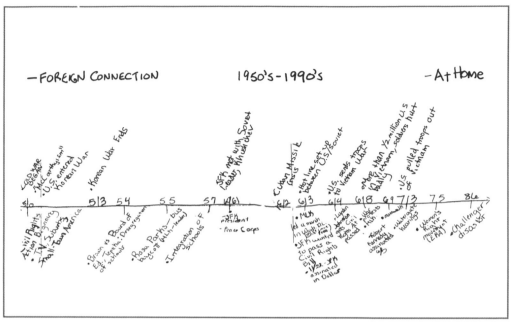

figure 6.2   Emily's time line depicting meaningful historical events occurring nationally or internationally.

"at home." She adds color as a key at the top of her page so that she can respond to the cues and categories of specific events. For example, all events occurring "at home" are written in pink and all events depicting the "foreign connection" are written in blue. Emily is pleased with her time line because she can use the content and her creativity to depict what she has learned. In cooperative group discussions, Pat guides children to examine time and sequence and encourages them to present their rationales for why they designed their time lines as they did (process), and why the information they selected depicts historical events (product).

• • • • • • • • • • • • • •

A Conceptual Organizer

Our next example of a graphic organizer in the area of social studies comes from Dana Roney-Nauerz, a teacher of middle-grade students. She and two other teachers, Penelope Koval and Doreen Saar, formed an interdisciplinary team to integrate the English and social studies content for their eighth grade students. Based on their own personal interest, they decided to focus their unit on the concept of conflict because they feel both children and adults face conflict in their lives on a daily basis. They also chose conflict because the concept is so central to both content areas.

As Dana puts it, "In the social studies curriculum, the idea of conflict relates the concepts of change, choice, diversity, culture, empathy, human rights, justice, and power. And in the English curriculum, conflict relates to the idea of literary conflict, one of the elements of literature required to be taught."

Figure 6.3 shows Dana, Penelope, and Doreen's plans for the unit. They believe strongly that students need to understand conflict in their own personal lives and that they need to know how to apply it to the broader spectrum of society. As you can see, this team of teachers want to promote both an understanding of the nature of conflict and an empathy for all people. The activities focus on students resolving conflicts internally and with one another. Dana, Penelope, and Doreen want each student to find peaceful solutions to problems, whether they occur in history or in literature. The key goal of their unit is to offer students flexibility, choice, and authenticity within each subject area so that they can develop the idea that people of all races and gender have dignity, rights, and worth.

● ● ● ● ● ● ● ● ● ● ● ● ● ● ● ●

Conflict Unit:

Organizing Ideas and Lesson Activities

1. All human beings deserve certain things. (Focused free-write and chart on human rights and needs; newspaper activity finding examples of human rights being violated.)
2. Conflict is a result of differences. (Continue newspaper activity; conflict analysis of Civil War, problem resolution in focused free-write.)
3. Without control we are helpless. (Active reading notation strategy on articles describing personal accounts of slavery; writing response on empathy; persuasive paper based on just treatment of others.)
4. Life is a constant struggle to solve problems. (Brainstorming

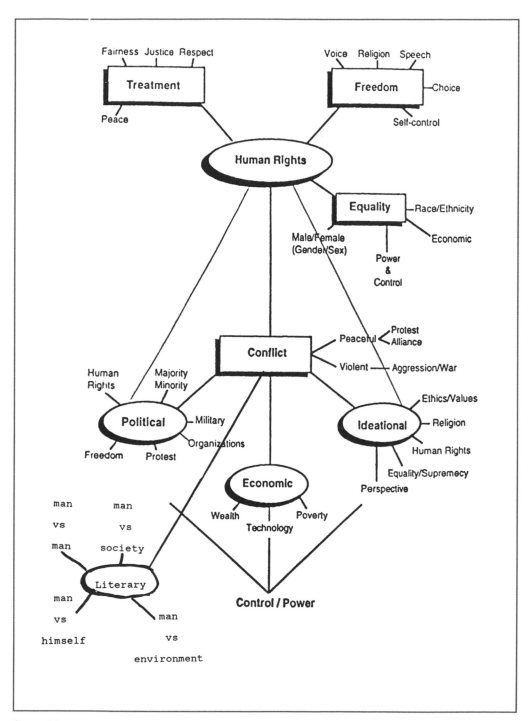

figure 6.3   An integrated English/social studies unit on the theme of "conflict."

on problem/conflict; explore literary conflict through Huck Finn excerpts and relate to social studies conflicts on the structured overview.)

5. We often take a stand for what we believe in. (Focused free-write on standing up for your own rights; read and analyze "The Ninny," which is about human rights.)

6. The struggle for freedom takes many forms. (Anticipation guide and levels guide on a reading about the civil rights movement, Martin Luther King, Jr., and Malcolm X.)

7. A picture is worth a thousand words. (Exploration of pictures as evidence of violation of human rights and pictures as modes of expression.)

8. Self-expression takes many forms. (Poetry analysis as it pertains to conflict and writing of poetry.)

9. Human rights are determined by those in a position of power. (Exploration of interview process; reading of an interview with Morris Dees, Jr.; prediction guide on hate crimes; human rights and white supremacy.)

10. An imbalance of power results in conflict and loss of human rights. (Card-sort review activity based on all concepts from unit; presentation of Individual Project Portfolios Assignment.)

● ● ● ● ● ● ● ● ● ● ● ● ● ● ●

A Hierarchical Organizer

A review of many social studies curriculum guides and syllabi shows that objectives for first grade frequently consist of helping children realize that they have roles as members of a family and school community. The development of identity and social interaction skills are stressed as students explore self, family, and school through these five perspectives: social, political, economic, geographic, and historic.

The graphic organizer in Figure 6.4 can be completed, over time, with the teacher as facilitator. Students who cannot yet write can illustrate each category and have the teacher act as scribe using children's words to explain their pictures. Students who write can use temporary spelling and complete the organizer in small cooperative groups or in pairs. A discussion can include the following understandings:

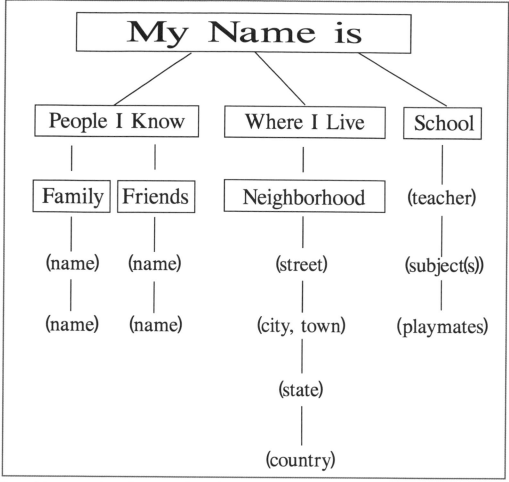

figure 6.4   A teacher-created graphic organizer for first graders to explore self, family, school, and community identity.

- Each person is unique.
- People live in families or family-like groups.
- Places can be located (on maps, globes, or by direction as relative to some other object).
- People, places and things change over time.

- People are alike and different in many ways although they share common characteristics, needs and wants.

The visual aide above, marked figure 6.4, helps first graders generalize that sharing, playing, and working with family,

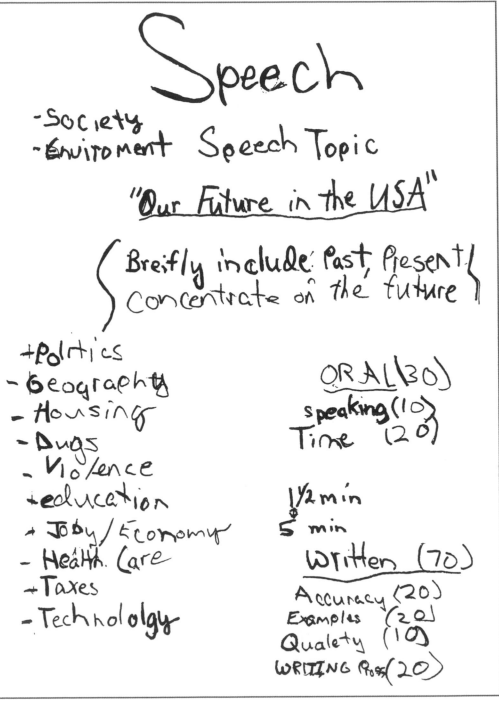

Speech

- Society
- Enviroment   Speech Topic

"Our Future in the USA"

{ Breifly include: Past, Present, concentrate on the future }

+ Poltics
- Geography
- Housing
- Dugs
- Violence
+ education
+ Joby / Economy
- Health Care
+ Taxes
- Technololgy

ORAL(30)
speaking (10)
Time (20)

1½ min
5 min
Written (70)

Accuracy (20)
Examples (20)
Qualety (10)
WRITING Pross (20)

figure 6.5   David's list of potential speech topics, along with oral and written criteria.

friends, and neighbors emphasize how special they are.

● ● ● ● ● ● ● ● ● ● ● ● ● ● ● ● ●

The Graphic Organizer as a Guide for Speaking

In "A SCANS Report for America 2000: What Work Requires of Schools," (U. S. Department of Labor, June 1991), speaking is identified as one of the key basic skills students will need for the future. This report defines speaking as "organizing ideas and communicating an oral message appropriate to listeners and situations." Speaking also includes participating in a conversation, or a discussion, or in a group or individual presentation.

David, an intermediate-grade student, selected the topic "Our Future in the USA" for a speech required in his social studies class. The speech, which he delivered to his peers and teacher, was the culminating activity for integrating language arts and the social studies content of recent American history. David's note (see Figure 6.5) includes his goals and a brainstormed list of topics as well as point distribution criteria for the written and oral speech. In Figure 6.6, you can see how David used a graphic organizer to collect his thoughts as he explored a narrower list of topics: environment, violence, drugs, and technology. David's essay (Figure 6.7) demonstrates how the graphic organizer assisted his creative thinking, problem solving, and decision making.

● ● ● ● ● ● ● ● ● ● ● ● ● ● ● ● ●

Conclusion

In the new design for social studies instruction, students will no longer "read the chapter and answer the questions at the end," as Garrett did. Teachers will encourage active learning, emphasize in-depth understanding, and utilize knowledge in complex situations, rather than expect rote responses from students.

The use of graphic organizers will assist teachers and their students to achieve both these essential skills and dispositions, as well as the standards put forth in the social studies frameworks of the future.

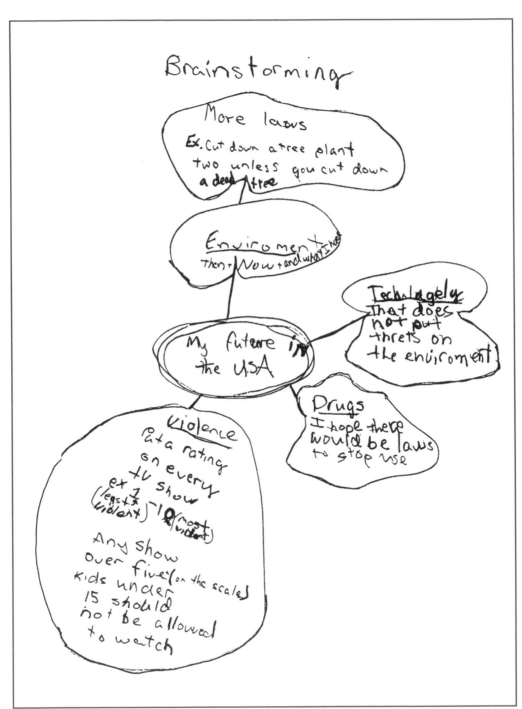

figure 6.6   David narrows his topic and gathers his thoughts for his speech by preparing this graphic organizer.

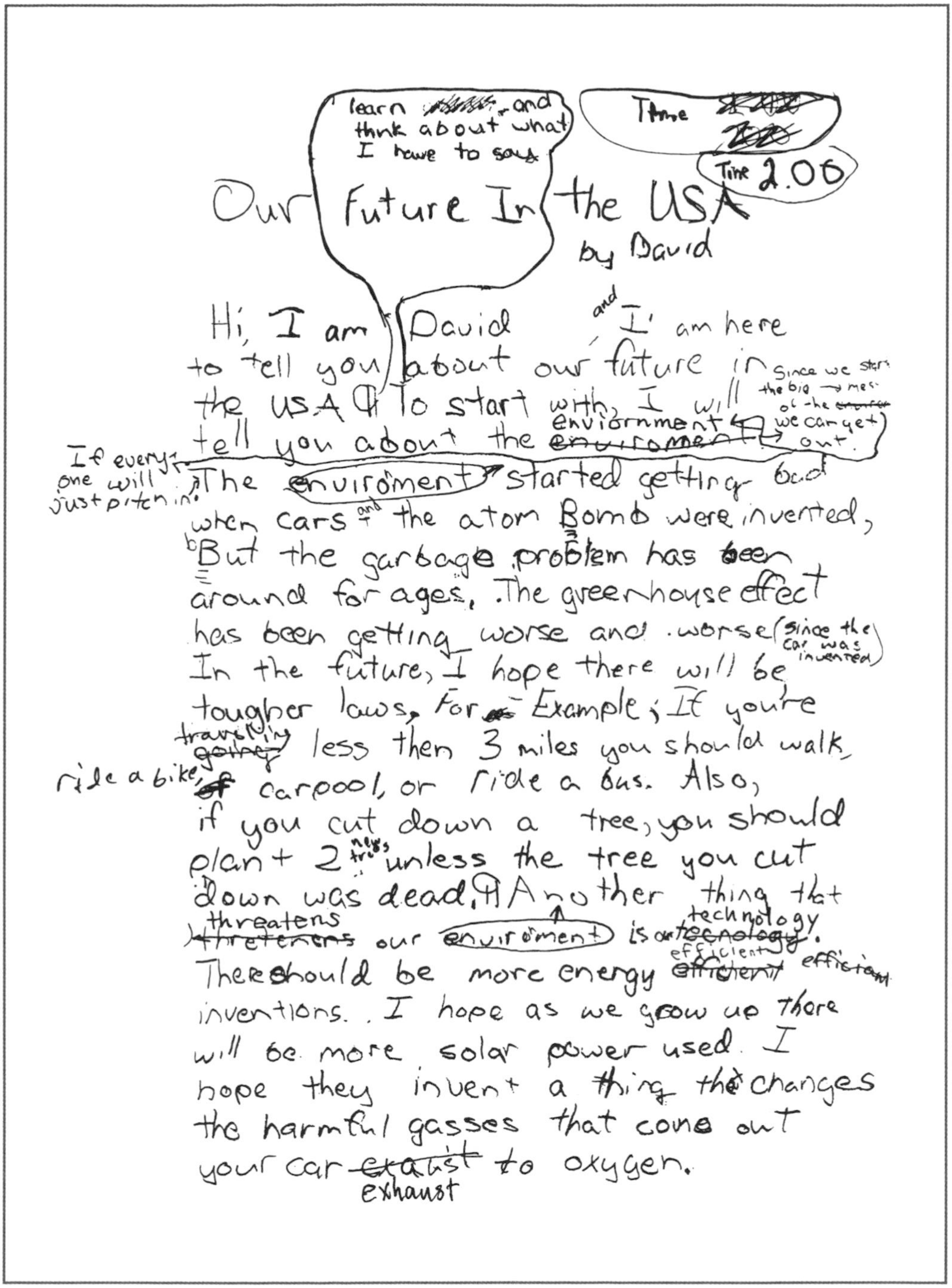
learn ~~[crossed out]~~ and think about what I have to say

Time ~~2:02~~ ~~2:00~~

Time 2.00

Our Future In the USA

by David

Hi, I am David and I am here to tell you about our future in the USA. ¶ To start with, I will tell you about the enviornment ~~enviroment~~ (Since we started the big mess of the ~~enviro~~ we can get out.)

If every one will just pitch in. The enviroment started getting bad when cars and the atom Bomb were invented, But the garbage problem has been around for ages. The greenhouse effect has been getting worse and worse (since the car was invented). In the future, I hope there will be tougher laws, For Example; If you're travelling ~~going~~ less then 3 miles you should walk, ride a bike, ~~or~~ carpool, or ride a bus. Also, if you cut down a tree, you should plant 2 new trees unless the tree you cut down was dead. ¶ Another thing that threatens ~~threteners~~ our enviroment is our technology ~~tecnology~~. There should be more energy efficient ~~efficient~~ efficiant inventions. I hope as we grow up there will be more solar power used. I hope they invent a thing that changes the harmful gasses that come out your car exhaust ~~exaust~~ to oxygen.

figure 6.7 A rough draft of David's speech reflects the topics he originally brainstormed and mapped.

Further Reading

Lunstrum, John P. and Taylor, Bob L. *Teaching Reading in the Social Studies*, Newark, DE: International Reading Association.

Parker, Walter C. *Renewing the Social Studies Curriculum*, Association for Supervision and Curriculum Development.

"What Work Requires of Schools: A SCANS Report for America 2000." June, 1991. U.S. Department of Labor.

Zarnowski, Myra and Gallagher, Arlene F. (Eds.). *Children's Literature and Social Studies: Selecting and Using Notable Books in the Classroom.* National Council for the Social Studies.

● ●

References

"Curriculum and Assessment Framework Sampler for Social Studies."1994. Albany, NY: State Education Department.

"Social Studies Program The University of New York." 1984. Albany, NY: State Education Department.

Questions & Answers

Are graphic organizers useful with non-English speaking students or ESL students?
Since graphic organizers can improve students' conceptual knowledge and vocabulary by focusing attention on key words and concepts, they are extremely useful for students whose first language is not English and non-native English speakers learning English. As students listen to and participate in the discussion that accompanies the development of an organizer, they begin to learn the concepts and accompanying English vocabulary. The creation of graphic organizers not only provides opportunities for the repetition of vocabulary, but also allows students to see how that oral language is represented in writing.

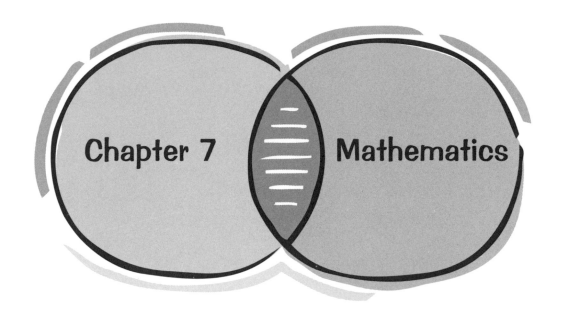

Chapter 7 — Mathematics

In *Notebooks of the Mind* (1985), Vera John-Steiner interviewed hundreds of creative people to determine their thinking processes. She found that many mathematicians and scientists, like Einstein, said they rely on visual symbols to think. John Howarth, a physicist engaged in cancer research, told John-Steiner: "I make abstract pictures...reduce the number of variables, simplify and consider what you hope is the essential part of the situation you are dealing with; then you apply your analytical techniques. In making a visual picture it is possible to choose one which contains representations of only the essential elements— a simplified picture, abstracted from a number of other pictures and containing their common elements" (pp. 84—85).

This link between visual thinking and scientific discovery is important to note here since, as we've stated, graphic organizers are visual representations of thought.

A glimpse into five classrooms where students and teachers use graphic organizers introduces you to a few of the ways this flexible tool supports effective thinking and instruction in mathematics.

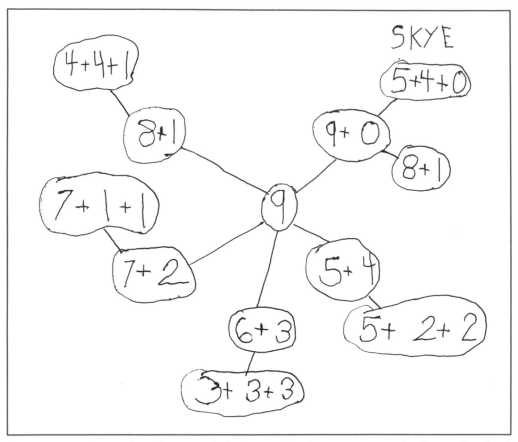

figure 7.1   A page from the journal of a first grader shows ways to make the number fact 9.

First Grade

Many first grade teachers understand that counting, numeration, addition, and subtraction are best developed through concrete activities. Teacher Elsa Bingel knows the value of having her students manipulate real objects and explore numbers in a variety of ways using many different materials. Her children not only learn counting and numeration, they also internalize the unique patterns and combinations each number forms naturally.

Elsa and other teachers like her also recognize the importance of having their students draw pictures of real objects or geometric shapes to show a variety of ways to represent numbers. As children become more proficient, Elsa leads them from concrete to abstract learning. They begin with manipulatives, then draw pictures, and finally begin to use numbers. For example, the graphic organizer in Figure 7.1 shows what Skye, a six-year-old, drew in her journal to show the number fact 9. Skye began with 9 in the center of the page and added the addition facts she knew that make nine (e.g., 4 + 5). Then she created three-factor number facts (e.g., 4 + 4 + 1) for these two-factor number facts. Skye said she created these facts in order from 9 to 5 "because it makes sense and you won't skip numbers that way." Making webs like this one can be a way for children to record their explorations with concrete objects, as well.

Creating graphic organizers to represent mathematical concepts and procedures helps students see relationships and connections among numbers. Too often, teachers neglect to use the strategy of drawing visual graphics as part of their math instruction. Teachers who do use graphic organizers in math know they need to model the procedure and use it regularly in their teaching before most of their students will use it confidently and effectively on their own.

In her first grade classroom, Elsa regularly uses different types of graphic organizers to depict numbers. She uses graphs like the ones in Figure 7.2 to help

figure 7.2 Elsa Bingel and her first graders created these graphs to keep track of birthdays and lost teeth.

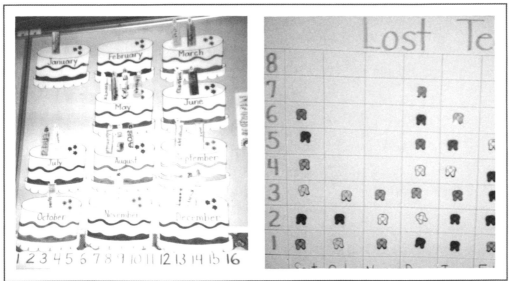

her children see relationships and organize information. Elsa uses the following steps to direct her first graders in their own research, data collection, and graph construction:

1. Ask a question.
2. Collect and organize information.
3. Record and label graph.

Like many primary teachers, Elsa and her children explore everyday topics such as the weather, days in a month, favorite foods, birthdays, and students' physical characteristics like hair and eye color. She and her children organize information using different types of graphs, including pie charts, scatter graphs, and bar graphs. This allows the children to see relationships, draw conclusions, and make predictions as they answer such questions as:

• How many ___ are there?
• Which column has the least (most)?
• Are there more (less)___ or more (less) ___?
• How many more (less) ___ are there than___?

• How many do you think there will be next time?

Elsa believes in using a wide assortment of materials and methods to help her children become flexible and creative thinkers as they experience different ways of arranging and organizing information. Graphic organizers are one of her most important tools.

● ● ● ● ● ● ● ● ● ● ● ● ● ● ●

Second Grade

Kim Ames, a second grade teacher, uses children's literature as a supplement to her school's math series. She knows the important role literature plays in teaching and reinforcing math concepts and computation skills. After attending an inservice workshop about the use of literature to teach mathematics, reading articles in professional journals, and enlisting the help of her school media specialist, Kim has collected many children's books that involve math and are written on a range of ability levels.

Kim finds that when she uses a graphic organizer to represent events and action in a story, two things occur. First, her stu-

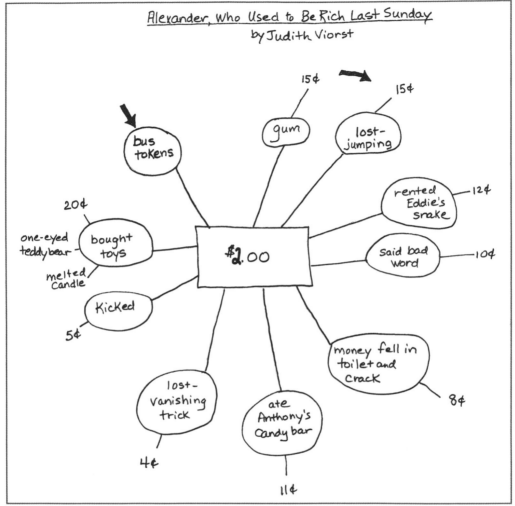

figure 7.3   A concept organizer created by Kim Ames to show how Alexander spent his money.

dents often understand the story better. Second, her students often use problem-solving skills and acquire math concepts as a direct result of their involvement with the story's characters and actions. For example, several of Kim's students had trouble with the addi- tion and subtraction of money, so she read *Alexander, Who Used to Be Rich Last Sunday* by Judith Viorst (Macmillan, 1980). In this humor- ous and realistic book, Alexander begins with $2.00 and either spends or loses his money by the end of the story. The first time Kim read this story to her children, she wanted them to enjoy it and respond to Alexander's plight. Only on rereading the story did Kim analyze it with her students in order to create the graphic organizer in Figure 7.3. Using this organizer to identify the amounts to be added helped Kim's students use computation to check Viorst's accuracy and to see how Alexander spent one of his dollars.

There are many children's books at all grade levels that you can link to your math teaching. There are stories that involve counting, computation, patterns and order classification, spatial relations, measurement, time, money, recording, and problem solving (Griffith & Clyne, 1988; Whitin & Wilde, 1992). After an initial reading for enjoyment and appreciation, these stories and the math concepts embedded in them are often clarified when you represent the content visually in some form of graphic organizer, as Kim did.

The following are titles of several picture books in which mathematical content is easily represented and reinforced by drawing a graphic organizer. You can share these books with stu-

dents to develop their understandings of a variety of math concepts:

1. *The Doorbell Rang* by Pat Hutchins (Morrow, 1989). Division and fractions are the focus as 2 children figure out how to share 12 cookies with their friends.

> **After an initial reading for enjoyment and appreciation, these stories and the math concepts embedded in them are often clarified when you represent the content visually in some form of graphic organizer.**

2. *Anno's Mysterious Multiplying Jar* by Mitsumasu and Masaichiro Anno (Putnam, 1983). Number patterns, multiplication, factorials, and estimation can be developed in this story about a magic jar that holds a sea, one island, and two countries, each of which holds three mountains, on each of

86

which are four kingdoms, with the pattern continuing.

3. *The Shopping Basket* by John Burningham (Harper, 1980). Counting, subtraction, patterns, spatial relations, and mapping are central to this story about a boy who goes shopping, has misadventures on his way home, and arrives with only a few of his purchases.

4. *Two Ways to Count to Ten* by Ruby Dee (Holt, 1988). Problem solving is the focus of this Liberian folktale in which King Leopard invites other animals to a spear-throwing contest to see who will marry his daughter and succeed him as King.

5. *Anno's Hat Tricks* by Mitsumasu Anno (Philomel, 1985). Logic and problem solving are developed in this story about three children who use binary logic and colors to solve a problem.

6. *Socrates and the Three Little Pigs* by Mitsumasu Anno (Philomel, 1986). Permutations and combinations are introduced in this story about Socrates, a wolf who looks for dinner for his wife Xanthippe.

7. *The King's Chessboard* by David Birch (Dial, 1988). The value of exponents and number expansion is explored in this ancient tale from India in which a proud king learns a lesson when he grants his wise man a special request.

These are only a few of the children's books available to you for enriching your teaching of mathematics. Your school library media specialist or the librarian in your public library can provide you with many other books appropriate to a range of grade levels and mathematics concepts.

There are also many current resources for teachers that link children's literature and mathematics. *Math Through Children's Literature* (Braddon, Hall, & Taylor, 1992) is one example.

Part 1 of this book explains the standards established by the National Commission on Teaching Mathematics (NCTM) and Part 2 contains summaries of trade books that relate to the first five NCTM standards.

● ● ● ● ● ● ● ● ● ● ● ● ● ● ● ●

Fourth Grade

In Doreen McSain's fourth grade, students often use "webs" to organize their knowledge of

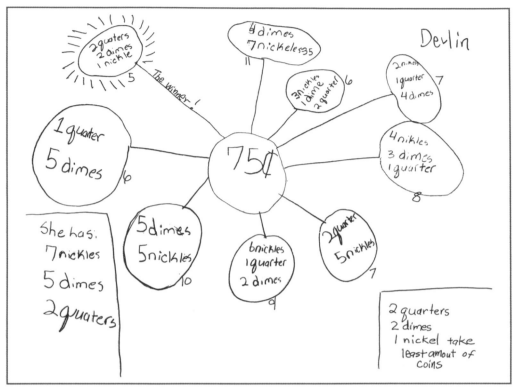

The web contains the following handwritten labels:

- **Devlin**
- 2 quaters 2 dimes 1 nickle — 5 — The winner!
- 4 dimes 7 nickeles 35
- 3 nickles 1 dime 2 quarter — 6
- 2 nickel 1 quarter 4 dimes — 7
- 4 nikles 3 dimes 1 quarter — 8
- 1 quarter 5 dimes — 6
- 75¢ (center)
- 5 dimes 5 nickles — 10
- 6 nickles 1 quarter 2 dimes — 9
- 2 quarter 5 nickles — 7
- She has: 7 nickles 5 dimes 2 quaters
- 2 quarters 2 dimes 1 nickel take least amout of coins

figure 7.4   Doreen McSain's fourth graders created webs like this one to help in problem solving.

concepts in reading and writing, and are beginning to use them in math.

To see how her students' understandings of a conceptual organizer might transfer to math, Doreen gave them the following problem and asked them to draw a map or web to help solve it:

"Maria wants to buy a 75-cent snack from a vending machine. The machine takes only nickels, dimes, and quarters. Maria has seven nickels, five dimes, and two quarters. Show all the different ways she could pay for the snack. Which of your ways uses the fewest number of coins?"

Doreen told her class that there are nine ways to solve the problem with exact change. Figure 7.4 shows the graphic organizer Devlin drew as he grappled with the problem.

To begin, Devlin listed Maria's coins on the bottom left corner of his paper and put 75¢ in a circle at the center of his paper.

Then he began to generate various combinations of coins to represent seventy-five cents, putting each in a circle that he connected to the center circle with a line.

Finally when Devlin had exhausted all the ways to combine the coins, he added the number of coins in each circle and wrote that number near that circle e.g., he wrote 7 near the circle that holds the words "1 quarter, 4 dimes, 2 nickels." Then, at a glance he knew that 5 was the fewest number and that circle held the answer, which he wrote at the bottom right corner of his paper.

Not all of her students were as successful in solving the problem as Devlin was, but Doreen concluded that concept mapping was helpful to many of them. In her words, "It helped them organize their thoughts while they were deciding what needed to be done, and it organized the work they did while they solved the problem. Using a web also gave them a specific place for their answers."

Based on the webs her students drew, Doreen knew that she needed to model the process with them and support them as they began to use webbing in problem solving.

Fifth Grade

Several of Kelly Haight's fifth graders had trouble reducing a fraction to its simplest form. Even after Kelly explained the process several times, these students could not grasp the concept. She realized she needed to simplify it, to show each step. It would also be important, she realized, to make the process visual and concrete.

Kelly's students were familiar with the Venn diagram, having used them in reading to compare and contrast stories and in social studies to compare regions of the world. So, Kelly decided to use a Venn diagram (Figure 7.5) to show her students how to determine the greatest common factor and reduce a fraction (18/30) in one step.

First, Kelly presented the fraction to be reduced. On one circle of the diagram, she wrote 18 and on the other she wrote 30. When students identified the largest factor of each, Kelly wrote 18 in one circle and 30 in the other. Next, she and her students began with 1 and proceeded through factors up to 18 and 30, deciding whether each number was a common factor, (to be recorded in the

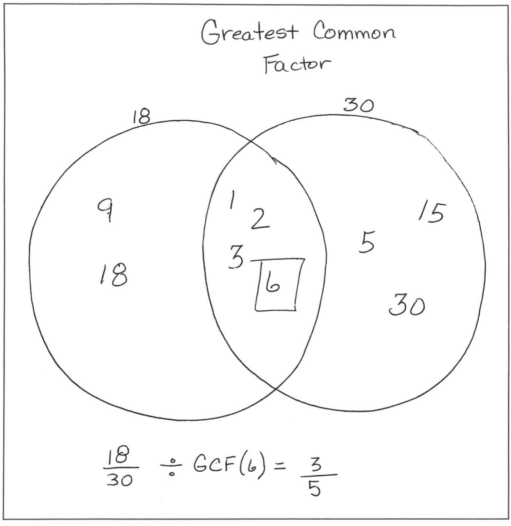

figure 7.5   Kelly Haight used this Venn diagram to show her fifth grade students a process for determining the greatest common factor to reduce a fraction.

overlap area of the two circles) or divisible only into 18 or 30, (recorded in the appropriate circle.) They identified 1, 2, 3, and 6 as common factors of both 18 and 30; 9 and 18 as factors of only 18, and 5, 15, and 30 as factors of only 30. In this way, the students could see the process for arriving at common factors as they recorded each factor on the graphic organizer.

For Kelly, the Venn diagram was an effective way to show her students how to find the greatest common factor. "Once they saw a visual representation of a 'greatest common factor' it was no longer an obscure three-word phrase but had become a number with a meaning," says Kelly. "They could use this number to reduce a fraction in only one step...they become more confident about reducing fractions."

This experience has made Kelly curious about other ways to use graphic organizers in math. One study found that self-generated drawings improved fifth graders' achievement on word-problem tests (Van Essen & Hamaker, 1994). Using a heuristic method like this, in which a drawing represents the structure of a problem, seemed to help these fifth graders analyze and work out word problems better. The results of this study have important implications for Kelly and other teachers at the intermediate level who may want to try using graphic organizers with their students as a heuristic to aid problem solving.

● ● ● ● ● ● ● ● ● ● ● ● ● ● ● ●

Eighth Grade

Eighth-grade math teacher, Colleen Murphy, often creates a graphic organizer to examine her own understanding of a mathematics concept before she begins teaching. "It helps me get organized and it's so logical to use." From the visual picture of mathematics content she creates, Colleen examines:

• The range of things she needs to teach.
• How various categories of information interrelate.
• How to teach the ideas and information in a connected way.

Creating a graphic organizer to represent your own content knowledge can help you be more thoughtful and effective in your teaching. This type of self-evaluation invites you to increase your understanding of the content and draws your attention to any gaps in your knowledge so that you can clarify your misunderstandings before you begin teaching.

Colleen also asks her students to create their own graphic organizers. She says, "A lot of students are visual learners. They like to see a picture and this gives them a picture of how concepts fit together." Colleen frequently shows her students one of her own graphic organizers or creates

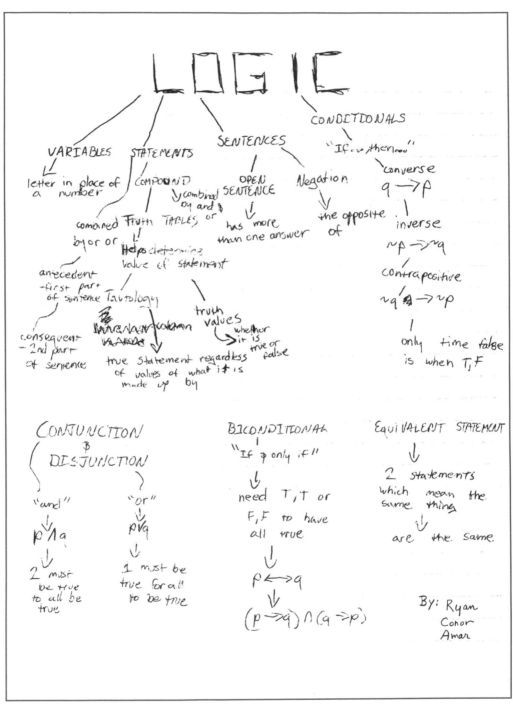

LOGIC

VARIABLES
↓
letter in place of a number

STATEMENTS
/
COMPOUND
↓ combined by and $
comaned by or or
↓
Truth TABLES
Help determining value of statement
/
Tautology
\
true statement regardless of values of what it is made up by

antecedent — first part of sentence

consequent — 2nd part of sentence

SENTENCES

OPEN SENTENCE
↓
has more than one answer

Negation
↓
the opposite of

truth values → whether it is true or false

CONDITIONALS
"If...then..."

converse
$q \rightarrow p$
|
inverse
$\sim p \rightarrow \sim q$
/
contrapositive
$\sim q \rightarrow \sim p$
|
only time false is when T, F

CONJUNCTION
&
DISJUNCTION

"and"
↓
$p \wedge q$
↓
2 must be true to all be true

"or"
↓
$p \vee q$
↓
1 must be true for all to be true

BICONDITIONAL
"If p only if"
↓
need T, T or F, F to have all true
↓
$p \longleftrightarrow q$
↓
$(p \rightarrow q) \wedge (q \rightarrow p)$

EQUIVALENT STATEMENT
↓
2 statements which mean the same thing
↓
are the same.

By: Ryan
Conor
Amar

figure 7.6   A hierarchical organizer for "Logic" created by Colleen Murphy's eighth graders.

one on the overhead projector to give them a model before they do their own. Her main focus in using graphic organizers with students is as a review tool. "It really helps them pull their ideas together," says Colleen. She often gives her students a list of words from a chapter they have just read and asks them to work in cooperative groups to constuct a graphic organizer.

Colleen often gives students the words printed on 3 x 5 cards so they can put the cards on the floor or a table top and manipulate them to determine the best configuration of ideas and information. She tells her students they can organize them any way they like as long as they have a logical rationale. Colleen says groups often structure information quite differently, with some students creating hierarchical organizers and others creating conceptual organizers. Finally, students either tape the cards onto chart paper or draw an organizer to represent their work. Three of Colleen's eighth grade students created the organizer in Figure 7.6.

When students finish their organizers, Colleen asks each group to present it to the rest of the class, explaining their organization and reasoning. The discussions that follow the presentations are lively; Colleen feels this is critical for the learning that occurs, because as students explain and defend their thinking, they learn to listen to others and often to rethink their assumptions. They learn to be flexible enough to revise their ideas when there is contradictory evidence and strong enough to stick to their convictions when the supporting evidence is convincing.

The process of student construction and explanation of graphic organizers gives Colleen important assessment information, too. What she learns about her students' knowledge guides her future teaching. In light of her students' achievement on tests and their personal responses to the strategy, Colleen believes creating graphic organizers is both a worthwhile and popular learning activity.

Undoubtedly, you will discover many other ways to use this flexible strategy to help your students succeed in their mathematics learning.

References

Braddon, K.L., Hall, N.J., & Taylor, D. (1992). *Math Through Children's Literature: Activities That Bring the New NCTM Standards Alive.* Englewood, CO: Libraries Unlimited/Teacher Ideas Press.

Griffith, R., & Clyne, M. (1988). *Books You Can Count On.* Portsmouth, NH: Heinemann.

John-Steiner, V. (1985). *Notebooks of the Mind:Explorations of Thinking.* New York: Harper & Row.

Van Essen, G., & Hamaker, C. (1994). "Using Self-generated Drawings to Solve Arithmetic Word Problems." *Journal of Educational Research*, 301–312.

Whitin, D.J., & Wilde, S. (1992). *Read Any Good Math Books Lately?* Portsmouth, NH: Heinemann.

Questions & Answers

Can parents work with students to create graphic organizers?

Yes, parental involvement in a student's school experience is always beneficial and working with a student to create graphic organizers is no different. Some parents may have expertise in "flow charting" or other types of graphic organizers in their work place, but for those who don't, we suggest reading about the why's and how's of graphic organizers or attending a workshop on them. If a workshop is not available, you can give parents detailed directions in a letter, or at a teacher-parent conference.

Are graphic organizers appropriate for students with diverse abilities and language backgrounds?

You will find that graphic organizers are an excellent instructional strategy for a wide range of students. Of course, you will want to be sure that you have provided appropriate modeling and practice and that the conceptual level of the organizer is appropriate for your students. You should also expect a range of responses that reflect the abilities and backgrounds of your students. By having your students work cooperatively to create and complete graphic organizers, you will enhance the learning, communication, and social skills of the students.

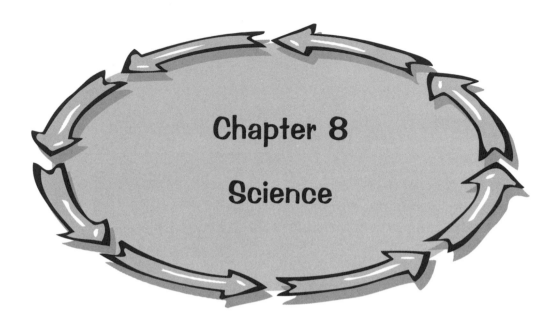

Chapter 8

Science

Scientists and science students are engaged in a process of inquiry about how the world works. They can use graphic organizers to show the relationships of scientific concepts and ideas. For example, sequence organizers can be used to represent problem-solution and cause-effect sequences; cyclical organizers can illustrate common cycles; and hierarchical organizers can depict catagorizations. These major ways of organizing knowledge are discussed in Chapter 1.

Research supports the use of graphic organizers to enhance learning in science. Hawk (1986) demonstrated that the use of graphic organizers improved the science achievement of middle school students. Levin et al., (1988) found graphic organizers were a helpful mnemonic strategy for learning botanical concepts. Lehman (1992) argues that graphic organizers are particularly effective in science classes with slower learners.

But whatever the needs, styles, and abilities of students, in science, as in other subject areas, graphic organizers prove to be useful tools. They aid in both the comprehension and recall of information.

Identifying Common Misconceptions Through Graphic Organizers

In science classrooms with students of diverse abilities, graphic organizers can be used as a prereading tool to help you identify the naive misconceptions many students have about the physical world. Barbara Lunn, an eighth-grade earth science teacher, often begins her units by having students brainstorm collaboratively to share what they already know about the topic. In this way Barbara helps activate students' prior knowledge, or schema, and encourages them to share information. This brainstorming also allows Barbara to see if there are any misconceptions about the topic that need to be addressed.

Much research supports Barbara's approach. Alvermann and Hynd (1989) found that "activating competent readers' naive conceptions about a complex scientific concept is not as effective a means for dispelling inaccurate information as is the practice of activating their naive conceptions and then explicitly directing them to read and attend to ideas that might be different from their own."

During the brainstorming session, Barbara puts the key concept in a circle on chart paper or on the overhead and then adds

> In science classrooms with students of diverse abilities, graphic organizers can be used as a prereading tool to help you identify the naive misconceptions many students have about the physical world.

information generated by the class—misconceptions and all. For example, after she introduced the topic, "Why does the earth have seasons?" students generated a collaborative map (Figure 8.1), that revealed their shared misconception that winter was colder because the earth was farther away from the sun than in summer. Barbara then tailored her instruction accordingly, telling students that as they read, they should look for information about the causes for the seasons in their

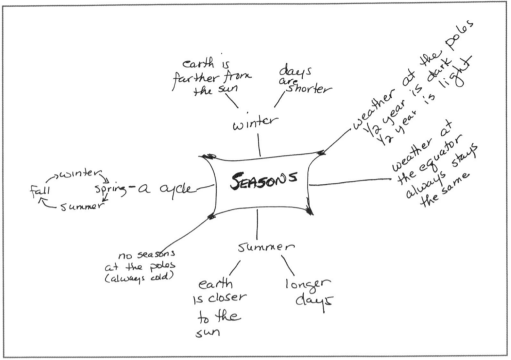

earth is farther from the sun

days are shorter

weather at the poles ½ year is dark ½ year is light

winter

weather at the equator always stays the same

winter
Fall
summer
spring – a cycle
SEASONS

no seasons at the poles (always cold)

summer
earth is closer to the sun

longer days

figure 8.1   A graphic organizer created by Barbara Lunn's eighth grade class depicts some misconceptions about the causes for seasonal weather differences.

reading and be especially alert for ideas which contradict their own notions of how the seasons are caused.

Deborah Pease took a different approach with her sixth graders. The class was beginning a unit on electrical devices for communication. Deborah had her students work individually to draw what they knew about how radios work. She asked the class, "What happens to the sound when someone sings a song in a radio station? How does the sound get from the radio station to your ears?" As the

students tried to depict the process visually, a number of questions and comments arose. In some cases, the students questioned each other, but more frequently they were wrestling with the questions themselves. They asked such questions as: Is there a wire? Magnetic waves...or is it? I really don't know how that happens. Kelly inquired, "Can I also write something to help explain my drawing?" Deborah said yes. She feels that the combination of prose and the graphic organizer is a good way to allow students to

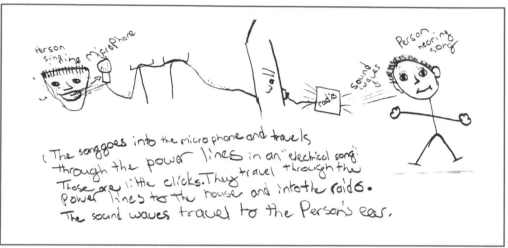

figure 8.2   Kelly's graphic organizer and written explanation of how radio waves are transmitted from the station to our ears.

draw on their individual strengths. Many students, like Kelly, will feel more comfortable if they can augment their visual organizers with narrative (Figure 8.2).

In examining the individual organizers, Deborah realized that, like Kelly, over one-third of the class—(including several students who were classified as learning disabled, but many more who were not)—thought that wires were used to convey radio waves. She knew she had to deal with this misconception explicitly in her instruction before any research or reading. By analyzing the individual graphic organizers, Deborah had an excellent grasp of each individual's prior knowledge. This information was help-

ful in setting up cooperative research groups. Deborah was able to insure that each group had at least one student who had a good grasp of the basic principles of the radio.

● ● ● ● ● ● ● ● ● ● ● ●

Children's Literature and Graphic Organizers

Using a combination of a trade book and a graphic organizer can be an excellent way to prepare students to read a science text or do an experiment. In Leigh's fifth-grade science class, the teacher, Michelle Haren, began by reading *A River Ran Wild* by Lynne Cherry (Harcourt Brace, 1992). After the class discussed the book briefly, groups of students completed a graphic organizer on the Nashua River that was arranged with a time line across the top and categories down the left side. (Figure 8.3) The activity provoked lively discussion for Leigh and the rest of her group about living in harmony with the earth and the more specific topic of water pollution in the Susquehanna River. In this way, the time line from *A River Ran Wild* combined with focused analysis, served as a motivating activity for a research project on local waterways and water pollution.

● ● ● ● ● ● ● ● ● ● ● ● ● ●

Planning and Recording Scientific Studies with a Vee Map

The Vee Map is another graphic organizer that can help students deal explicitly with what they already know, the questions they have, and what they find out

figure 8.3   A fifth grade class collaborated to complete this time line matrix based upon Lynn Cherry's *A River Ran Wild,*; teacher Michelle Haren created the matrix.

NASHUA RIVER

	1400	1600	1850	1960	1994
People	Pennacook tribe – Native Americans	Massachusetts Colonists	European Immigrants		Environmentalists
River	clear, clean, wild	dams, ponds, floating logs	Sewerage, waste, pulp, dye, chemicals, clogged, terrible stench		clear, clean
Riverbank	forests, small clearings, thatched houses cattails, few crops	cleared fields fenced pastures	factories, plants, mills		homes, replanted forests
Aquatic (water) life	fish, beaver, turtles, salmon	fish, beaver, turtle, salmon	no life		return of fish, beaver turtles
River valley wildlife	deer, geese, hawks, owls	fewer numbers of wildlife because of hunting	wildlife scarce due to illness from pollution and hunting		return of wildlife in many areas (protected)

from *A River Ran Wild* by Lynne Cherry

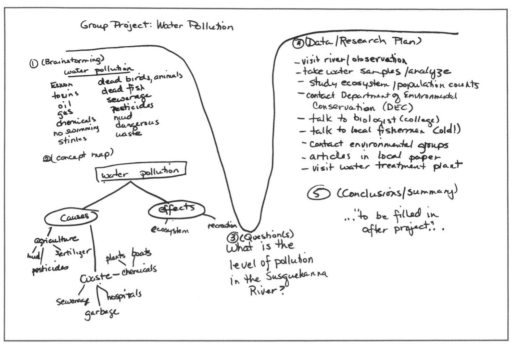

Group Project: Water Pollution

① (Brainstorming)
water pollution

Exxon   dead birds, animals
toxins   dead fish
oil   sewerage
gas   pesticides
chemicals mud
no swimming dangerous
stinks   waste

② (concept map)

| water   pollution |

Causes   Effects
                    ecosystem   recreation
agriculture
mud/ fertilizer
pesticides   plants boats
           Waste — chemicals
    sewerage / hospitals
       garbage

④ (Data / Research Plan)
- visit river / observation
- take water samples / analyze
- study ecosystem / population counts
- contact Department of Environmental
     Conservation (DEC)
- talk to biologist (collage)
- talk to local fishermen (old!)
- contact environmental groups
- articles in local paper
- visit water treatment plant

⑤ (Conclusions / summary)
  ..."to be filled in
     after project"...

③ (Question(s)
What is the
level of pollution
in the Susquehanna
River?

figure 8.4   A Vee Map completed by Leigh's fifth grade research group as they planned
               a project on water pollution in the Susquehanna River.

from their experiments. Roth and Verechaka (1993) suggest the Vee Map as a way of depicting what students know and the "route to new and future knowledge. " (p. 25). Leigh's group used the Vee Map (Figure 8.4) to plan their project on the health of the Susquehanna River. On the left side of the map, students recorded the words they already knew about water pollution. After listing the terms, the group used a concept map to show the relationships among them. In the center of the map, they recorded their focus question. For Leigh's group the question was, "What is the current state of pollution of the Susquehanna River?" At the top right of the Vee Map, the group listed the events, experiments, and resources that they identified to answer their focus question. On the bottom right side of the map, Leigh's group will record the results of the research, their analysis, and conclusions. The Vee Map provides valuable assistance in helping Michelle's students plan systematic research that proceeds from their own background knowledge and builds new learning by way of a focused inquiry.

Using a Matrix to Record Data

In addition to identifying prior knowledge and common misconceptions, it's beneficial to actively involve students in experimenting and hypothesizing. This inquiry-based approach lends itself well to a type of graphic organizer called a matrix. A matrix is a visual presentation of a number of categories that are compared by looking at key variables. For example, Deborah Pease created the matrix in Figure 8.5 for a sixth grade science experiment. This matrix on static electricity helped Deborah's students to organize and record the information they generated as they did experiments. Looking at the information in this way facilitated the formulation of hypotheses, such as:

• **Kelly:** "The wool stuck the longest for me. I think that's because the rubbing of the balloon on the rough wool made the most ions. The two balloons repelled because they had the same charges."

figure 8.5   John, a sixth grader, completed this matrix on static electricity. The matrix was created by his teacher, Deborah Pease.

NAME John — STATIC ELECTRICITY OBSERVATIONS

MATERIALS / OBSERVATIONS	COTTON	HAIR	LEATHER	SILK	WOOL	2 WOOL-RUBBED BALLOONS	Other: Jeans
Strong Attraction	60 sec. +	20 sec. +	80 sec. +	90 sec. +	120 sec +	—	90 sec. +
Medium Attraction	—	—	—				—
Weak Attraction			—	—	—		—
No Attraction	—	—	—	—	absolute repel +		—

John, great ideas!

Hypothesis: ① the more ruf a piece of cloth is the longer it holds
② The longer you rub the balloon against the cloth the longer it holds.
③ Where you put the balloon to see if it holds will
+ Observed   also have an effect on the hold of the balloon
④ If the hold is strong you should be able to feel a
− Not observed force of attraction.

• **Kerri:** "My hair stuck the best. I think it was because it is short and fuzzy. My hair probably took almost all the electrons from the balloon creating an ion."

Because the matrix presents information in such a structured, visual way, it is an excellent tool to help students identify patterns and relationships. Finding these patterns and relationships is central to the generation of hypotheses that can be used to clarify past experiences and guide further experiments. The static electricity matrix activity provoked Kristen to share and interpret a past experience:

"At my babysitter's house I was playing with my best friend and when I touched her I got a shock. This happened when I went across the rug really fast and shook the electrons and protons out of place. This is called static electricity. Another experience was when I got the laundry out of the dryer."

Using Graphic Organizers as Study and Research Guides

When Pat Lynch's third grade class began a unit about tropical rain forests, Pat created a matrix based upon the various levels of the rain forest and some key variables within each level. This matrix served as a study guide as her students read and researched in cooperative groups. After each group completed its matrix, the class negotiated a single matrix on the overhead projector. Pat reproduced the matrix (Figure 8.6) on the computer so that each student could have a copy.

A number of issues came up as the students negotiated the rain forest matrix. Students explored word choices as they identified common ideas and synonyms. "Damp," "wet," and "humid" were mentioned as characteristics of the rain-forest floor. The students decided that they all had the same basic idea, but that *humid* was the best word to convey that idea.

A lively discussion ensued as students tried to differentiate between the amount of sunlight in

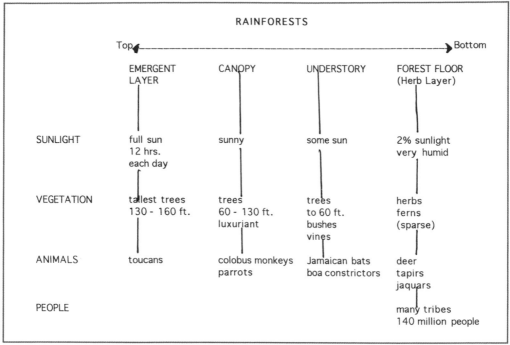

RAINFORESTS

	EMERGENT LAYER	CANOPY	UNDERSTORY	FOREST FLOOR (Herb Layer)
SUNLIGHT	full sun 12 hrs. each day	sunny	some sun	2% sunlight very humid
VEGETATION	tallest trees 130 - 160 ft.	trees 60 - 130 ft. luxuriant	trees to 60 ft. bushes vines	herbs ferns (sparse)
ANIMALS	toucans	colobus monkeys parrots	Jamaican bats boa constrictors	deer tapirs jaguars
PEOPLE				many tribes 140 million people

figure 8.6   A computer copy of a matrix on rain forests completed by Pat Lynch's third grade class.

the canopy and the understory. In order to clarify their ideas, students consulted the texts, trade books, and other resources.

When Pat asked the class how they liked the process of generating the class matrix, the students responded enthusiastically:

Matt: "We had the same words, but on this we had to come up with our ideas..."
Nick: "Talking with the other groups helped us expand our ideas."

Garrett: "Some people had things you hadn't thought of."

Students should be encouraged to discuss the rationale for their choices of categories and variables. Eventually, they should be able to examine science content independently, and from that content determine appropriate categories and variables. The process of creating graphic organizers not only leads to a greater understanding of the content, but also the organizer itself is a valuable guide for review and study.

Categorizing Information with Graphic Organizers

Marilew Bartling's first graders were learning about pets. Marilew put the word *pets* in a circle on the board and began to make a concept web by adding all of the pets the group named. Then Marilew asked the group to think of types of pets. Pace immediately volunteered, "Animals." Beth called out, "Fish." Marilew then guided a discussion of what pets belonged in each category, and when "parakeet" did not fit either of the two categories, the third category of "birds" was added. Says Marilew:

"Graphic organizers are an excellent tool to help children understand the concept of categorizing. The students have already practiced categorizing with real objects in kindergarten. I begin using a felt board early in the year so that students can group the felt pieces by their attributes. Even when students have moved from categorizing objects and pictures to words, they still need to see the information in a visual way. Graphic organizers are a logical way to do that."

Beyond categorization, graphic organizers can be used for the following purposes:

• **Before reading/research.** Use them to identify students' prior knowledge of the topic; enable students with diverse experiences to share information and provide everyone with some common background; highlight naive misconceptions that you should address directly; relate the topic to the students' own interests and needs; and assist students in setting up a plan for research.

• **During reading/research.** Use graphic organizers to guide reading and highlight important ideas; depict visually the way information is organized; and provide a format for recording information as it is located or generated.

• **After reading/research.** Use them to categorize concepts, ideas, and information; demonstrate students' comprehension and retention of key concepts and their interrelationships; facilitate the formation of hypotheses by presenting information in a highly organized way; provide an effective study guide for review; assess students' learning; compare students' understanding before and after reading/research; and identify areas that need reteaching and/or further research.

By using a variety of graphic organizers to meet a range of needs, you can enhance students' understanding of their world and provide a valuable tool for independent learning.

● ●

References

Alvermann, D. & Hynd, C. (1989). "Effects of Prior Knowledge Activation Modes and Text Structure on Nonscience Majors' Comprehension of Physics." *Journal of Educational Research*, 83, (2), 97-102.

Butzow, C. & Butzow, J. (1989). "Science Through Children's Literature. Englewood, CO: Teacher Ideas Press.

Hawk, P. (1986). "Using Graphic Organizers to Increase Achievement in Middle School Life Science." *Science Education*, 70, (1), 81-87.

Lehmann, H. (1992). Graphic organizers benefit slow learners. Clearinghouse, 66, (1), 53-55.

Levin, M., et al. (1988). "Mnemonic Text-Processing Strategies: A Teaching Science for Science Teaching." *Reading Psychology*, 9, (4), 343-363.

Roth, W. & Verechaka, G. (1993). "Plotting a Course with Vee Maps." *Science and Children*, January, 1993, 24-27.

Saul, W. & Jagusch, S. (1991). *Vital Connections: Children, Science and Books*. Portsmouth, NH: Heinemann.

Questions & Answers

Can the computer be a tool for creating graphic organizers?

Yes, both teachers and students can produce graphic organizers on the computer using a variety of software. The graphic organizers that are generated have a professional quality and can be edited with ease. Also, these graphic organizers can be stored on a disk for later reference, revision, or study which is one advantage of using this technology. Another advantage of computer-generated graphics is that students who lack interest and motivation for traditional writing and study tasks are often excited about using the computer. When these students learn to use the appropriate software, they create excellent graphic organizers.

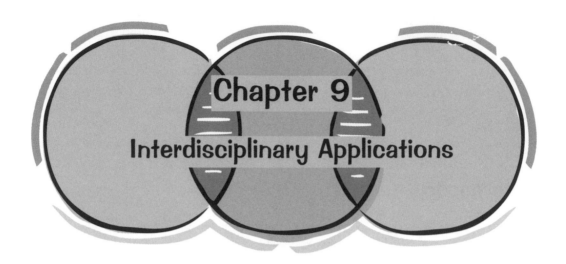

Chapter 9
Interdisciplinary Applications

Many teachers are exploring interdisciplinary approaches to curriculum, either individually, or in teams. Teachers in elementary and middle schools have often promoted interdisciplinary teaching, usually centered around themes. With the acceptance of the middle school philosophy that stresses collaborative problem solving in real-world contexts, there is an even greater emphasis on interdisciplinary curriculum for young adolescents. Jacobs (1989) defines the interdisciplinary approach as:

A knowledge view and curriculum approach that consciously applies methodology and language from more than one discipline to examine a central theme, issue, problem, topic, or experience (p. 8).

There are a number of advantages to interdisciplinary approaches to curriculum (Jacobs, 1989; Brandt, 1991; Kovalik, 1993). Interdisciplinary approaches:

• Reduce the artificial fragmentation of curriculum
• Help students see the relevance of their learning

- Clarify links among fields of knowledge
- Explore ideas and problems in context
- Encourage students to examine issues through a variety of disciplinary approaches
- Foster the cooperation of teachers in cooperative settings
- Allow students to gain understandings that would rarely be possible in a discipline-based approach
- Maximize valuable time by integrating disciplines
- Support problem-solving activities organized thematically

● ● ● ● ● ● ● ● ● ● ● ● ● ● ● ● ●

Choosing Among the Approaches to Curriculum Organization

Interdisciplinary curriculum occurs in many shapes and forms. Teachers who have their own classrooms have flexibility and control, but they often bear the full weight of interdisciplinary cur-

riculum development. When teachers collaborate in teams, the amount of common planning time, flexibility of schedule, physical facilities, and mandated curriculum are important considerations in choosing the specific interdisciplinary approach.

> **Teachers and students need to clarify their understandings through dialogue, and often such discussion leads to expansion or modifications that improve the organizer, the interdisciplinary unit, and the learning that occurs.**

Students' backgrounds, interests, learning styles, and expertise in cooperative and collaborative learning are also important factors to consider.

Jacobs (1989) describes a number of options for designing curriculum (pp. 13—18). Each option has its own advantages and drawbacks.

Curriculum Options

• **Discipline-based.** The traditional approach treats each discipline separately. There is no integration.

• **Parallel.** Lessons are sequenced so that they correspond with other disciplines. Native American history is taught in social studies at the same time as students read *Knots on a Counting Rope* by Bill Martin, Jr., and John Archambault (Holt, 1990) in language arts.

• **Multidisciplinary.** This is the thematic approach. Related disciplines are brought together to focus on a theme or issue. For example, science and technology teachers plan a unit on airplanes that includes basic aerodynamic principles, history of aviation, and aircraft design.

• **Interdisciplinary.** This approach attempts to bring together the full array of discipline-based perspectives. An example is a unit on change that includes activities from all of the elementary-school curricular strands.

• **Integrated day.** This is a child-centered curricula built on the child's interests and needs. This approach is most commonly found in pre-schools.

• **Complete day.** This is a totally integrated program. One of the rare examples of this approach is Summerhill. At Summerhill, education and school are totally integrated; they are life for the students and faculty who board there.

Each of these options is appropriate at various times and for a variety of purposes. Jacobs (1991) cautions that: "The biggest obstacle to interdisciplinary curriculum planning is that people try to do too much at once. What they need to look for are some, not all, natural overlaps between subjects. When studying the Renaissance, it just makes sense to include the literature, the social studies, the art, the music. It may not make sense to try and put in a lot of science.

Certainly, if you are just beginning to use interdisciplinary approaches, you would be wise to begin with a few units that combine some of the disciplines for a relatively short period of time. As you and your fellow teachers and students become more comfortable, you may wish to plan more inclusive and lengthier units.

Graphic organizers are excellent tools for interdisciplinary planning, teaching, learning, and assessment. Because so much of the emphasis of interdisciplinary curriculum is on substantive connections, graphic organizers are a natural tool: They depict visually the way in which knowledge is connected within and among disciplines.

Whether the graphic organizer is a teacher planning tool or a student guide to the content, discussion of the concepts and connections depicted in the organizer is critical. Teachers and students need to clarify their understandings through dialogue. It is often such discussion that leads to the expansions or modifications that improve the organizer, the interdisciplinary unit, and the learning that occurs.

● ● ● ● ● ● ● ● ● ● ● ● ● ● ● ●

Supporting Brainstorming Across Disciplinary Boundaries

The example in figure 9.1 is a reproduction of a graphic organizer created by a team of eighth graders when they were asked to brainstorm ideas around the theme of Heroes. This activity served to motivate the students and activate their prior knowledge about heroes and the values they consider "heroic".

Students were quick to name a variety of public figures from politics, business, entertainment, and sports, as well as historical and fictional heroes. As students contributed names to the list, they began to question the definition of a hero and to examine the differences between a hero and a celebrity. A number of students commented that they did not think there were any present-day heroes.

Using the information in the graphic organizer titled "Heroes" as a starting point, eighth grade teachers Cathy Lynch and Bonnie Slentz designed a unit to integrate social studies and language arts.

The organizing idea was "Heroes mirror a society's values." Cathy and Bonnie used the graphic organizer and their state-mandated curriculum to plan a number of activities for their heterogeneous team of 60 eighth-graders. The activities were designed to explore heroes of the past and present as they reflect the values of their day.

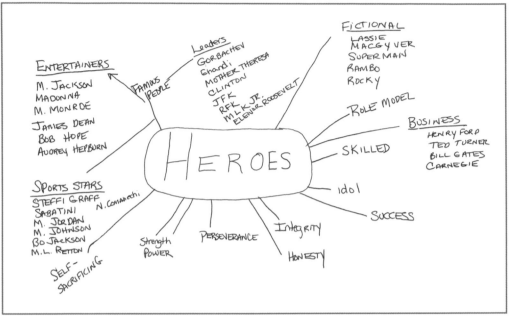

figure 9.1   A graphic organizer on heroes created by the eighth grade class of Cathy Lynch and Bonnie Slentz.

Seeing Connections and Clarifying Concepts

Using fiction, biography, and historical accounts, students explored the heroes of other cultures, of our American past, and the current day. By focusing on the way in which society's values were mirrored in its heroes, students were able to make connections across the disciplines. Comparing the values of Ghandi and Martin Luther King using a Venn diagram led the team to a greater understanding of the similarities and differences of India under British rule and of African Americans in the years prior to the civil rights movement.

Halley, one of the eighth graders working with Cathy and Bonnie, was inspired by the quiet heroism in *Anne Frank: The Diary of a Young Girl*. (Doubleday, 1952). For her major project, she chose to contrast the values that sustained Anne through her ordeal with those of Zlata Filipovic, the young Bosnian author of *Zlata's Diary: A Child's Life in Sarajevo* (Viking, 1993). Halley chose to use a Venn diagram to look at the ways in which the cultures and values of Anne and Zlata were alike and the ways in which they were different. She drew upon her historical research as well as the autobiographical information. In her concluding comments, Halley writes:

"I was amazed that the values of Anne and Zlata were so similar, but their values were not respected by the leaders of their countries. Maybe kids can be heroes, but why don't older people listen to them and share their values?"

Cathy and Bonnie were both delighted with their integrated unit. Their students had demonstrated substantative understanding of the interconnectedness of the curriculum areas addressed.

They planned a debate for the culminating activity. The debate question was: "Resolved: There are no heroes in 1994." The question arose from the discussion that accompanied the initial graphic organizer. The students were able to connect historical and fictional heroes to their own lives and explore values in ways that made the learning much more interesting and relevant.

Facilitating Formal Planning

Graphic organizers can be used for more formal interdisciplinary planning, as well. This formal planning occurs when teams of teachers choose to do team, grade-level, or school-wide planning. When teams of teachers are collaborating, graphic organizers are a clear and concise way to organize information and ideas from a number of perspectives and disciplines and to insure a balanced and meaningful integration of the disciplines. Figure 9.2 is an example of a primary integrated unit on change. Developed by a team of three teachers, Lucy Kelly, Connie Moxley, and Lynda Race, the unit was designed for a multi-age team of primary children who ranged in age from five to nine. The organizing idea for the unit was "I am changing and the world is changing around me." It includes learning opportunities from a wide range of disciplines. In planning the unit, the organizer helped these teachers explore a broad range of disciplines, look for meaningful connections, and balance activities so that no area is neglected or over represented.

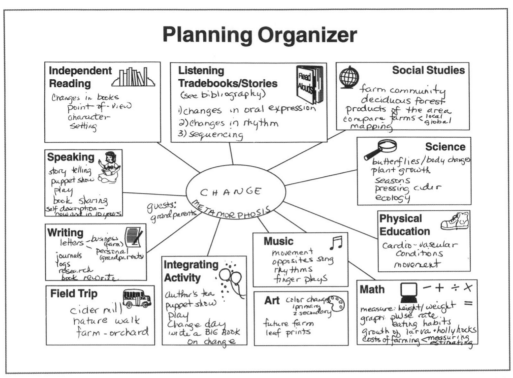

Planning Organizer

Independent Reading
Changes in books
point-of-view
character-
setting

Listening Tradebooks/Stories
(see bibliography)
1) changes in oral expression
2) changes in rhythm
3) sequencing

Social Studies
farm community
deciduous forest
products of the area
compare farms < local/global
mapping

Speaking
story telling
puppet show
play
book sharing
self description —
now and in 10 years

Science
butterflies/body change
plant growth
seasons
pressing cider
ecology

CHANGE
METAMORPHOSIS
guests:
grandparents

Physical Education
cardio-vascular
conditions
movement

Writing
letters — business (farm)
personal (grandparents)
journals
logs
research
book rewrite

Integrating Activity
author's tea
puppet show
play
change day
write a BIG Book
on change

Music
movement
opposites song
rhythms
finger plays

Math
measure: height/weight
graph pulse rate
eating habits
growth of larva + hollyhocks
costs of farming < measuring/estimating

Field Trip
cider mill
nature walk
farm - orchard

Art
color change
1 primary
2 secondary
future farm
leaf prints

figure 9.2   A graphic organizer for a primary interdisciplinary unit on change created by Lucy Kelly, Connie Moxley, and Lynda Race.

Often teachers use a web to organize the resources that are available for an interdisciplinary unit. Books, speakers, field trips, software, literature, equipment, and manipulatives are documented on a graphic organizer to facilitate planning. This is particularly helpful when teachers from a number of disciplines collaborate, as the collective knowledge of teachers with different areas of expertise supports a rich and varied set of resources to support the unit. As well, these resources may be used judiciously to support a number of objectives and avoid duplication.

Guiding Students' Interdisciplinary Explorations

Graphic organizers are appropriate guides for students' explorations. A KWHL organizer can help students understand what they know (K), what they

Paper Mills: Environment and the Economy			
K	**W**	**H**	**L**
WHAT I WANT TO KNOW	WHAT I WANT TO LEARN	HOW AM I GOING TO LEARN	WHAT DID I LEARN; WHAT DO I STILL WANT TO KNOW
-smells bad, like rotten eggs -pollutes air and water -uses trees -employs a lot of people - makes money	-what things are they putting in our water and air -why does it smell like that? -do they recycle or use recycled paper -how do you measure pollution -are there laws and fines -what would happen to the town and the people if the mill closed -what do the mayor and the other politicians say about it -how does it affect plants, animals... and humans -how paper is made (can we do it?)	-field trip to mill -field trip to Pigeon River -interviews -photographs -library -newspaper and magazine articles -guest speakers from the Wildlife and Environmental Agencies -visit a water analysis lab -Chamber of Commerce -do a water analysis -try making paper	

*based upon J. Williams and T. Reynolds (1993). Courting controversy: How to build interdisciplinary units. Educational Leadership, 50, 7, 13-15.

figure 9.3   A KWHL organizer based upon an interdisciplinary unit on paper mills (Williams & Reynolds, 1993).

want to learn (W), how they might learn what they want to know (H), and finally what they have learned and still want to know (L). The KWHL organizer in Figure 9.3 is based upon an interdisciplinary unit completed by sixth graders from Asheville, North Carolina (Williams & Reynolds, 1993). This organizer provides an overview of an interdisciplinary unit on paper-mills, a relevant and controversial topic in a nearby Tennessee community.

The students and teachers who planned and implemented

this unit were able to include their disciplines in real and relevant ways to support what the students wanted to learn. Science activities focused on river pollution and the waste products of the paper mill. Students learned about water-sampling techniques and the technology available for monitoring stream pollution. The social studies teacher used a current events approach to explore issues of toxic waste, the local economy, environmental concerns, and the political situation. The language arts teacher was delighted at the opportunity to have students reading, writing, speaking, and listening in authentic contexts. Students researched through reading, interviews, and role playing. They wrote reports, position papers, and interview write-ups. Mathematics was included as students manipulated the data gathered during water sampling. Calculations included depth and temperature. Students also collected, budgeted, and managed the money for their field trip to the paper mill. The KWHL organizer is an effective visual tool for teachers who are looking for meaningful, relevant connections among their disciplines based upon the interests of their students.

Evaluating Interdisciplinary Designs

Graphic organizers are also helpful in alleviating some of the concerns about interdisciplinary curriculum. You can evaluate your plans by using the graphic organizer to answer the following questions (Roth, 1994; Jacobs, 1989):

• Does the theme justify the amount of time needed for the unit?
• Does the unit focus on powerful ideas or organizing concepts that are important to the disciplines and appropriate for our students?
• Is our enthusiasm for the topic overshadowing what is most important for our students to understand?
• Does the graphic organizer have "forced" rather than "natural" connections among the disciplines?
• Will our students be able to transfer knowledge from one discipline to another?

- Does the unit overemphasize one discipline at the expense of others?
- Does the theme or focus enrich our students' understanding in each of the disciplines?

● ● ● ● ● ● ● ● ● ● ● ● ● ● ● ●

Recognizing and Celebrating Students' Diverse Interests and Talents

Graphic organizers also support teachers' attempts to implement learning and instructional theory as they plan interdisciplinary units. Art teacher Virginia Hawkins and the other teachers on her team created a graphic organizer that uses Gardner's theory of multiple intelligences (1983). Gardner theorizes that there are seven major types of intelligence: verbal-linguistic, logical-mathematical, visual, bodily-kinesthetic, interpersonal, intrapersonal and musical-rhythmic. Virginia and her team decided to shape an integrated curriculum based upon these aspects of intelligence and focused on the concept of balance. By planning a thematic unit on balance in this way, Virginia and her colleagues validate the wide spectrum of their students' talents.

As Virginia's team explored the issue of balance, they agreed on a number of curricular areas that would be the responsibility of a specific teacher. They also found areas that were natural for collaboration. For example, Virginia and the language arts teacher decided to look at balance in advertising between the visual and the verbal messages being communicated. Thus, they covered the visual and verbal-linguistic aspects of intelligence. The teachers of science, technology, and mathematics agreed to team for a special emphasis on weights and measures to emphasize the concept of balance. This collaboration emphasized the logical-mathematical intelligence of students and also involved verbal and bodily intelligence. In band classes the music teacher helped students understand the balance among the instruments in the orchestra. The health teacher worked with students to explore their beliefs and attitudes about the balance of freedom and responsibility in mature sexuality (intrapersonal intelligence). All teachers agreed to

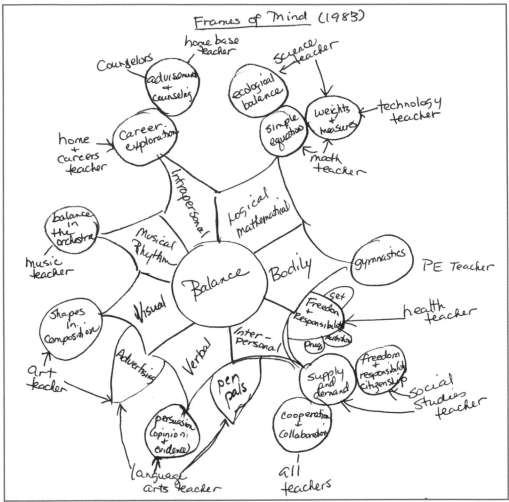

figure 9.4   A graphic organizer created by Virginia Hawkins and based upon Gardner's Multiple Intelligences as applied to the theme of "Balance."

work on interpersonal intelligence by helping students achieve appropriate balance in their cooperative and collaborative groups. They decided to emphasize turn-taking, shared leadership, and gender equity. Virginia's team found that by looking at curriculum in this way, they were able to make connections between and among disciplines and find natural areas for collaboration. Virginia speaks of her traditional experiences compared with this more interdisciplinary approach: "I see a major difference in the philosophy underlying the two approaches. Option A (the traditional curriculum) is really making a patchwork of learning experiences. Option B (interdisciplinary curriculum) is more wholistic and integrated. It implies an understanding of the connections among concepts and processes."

Virginia frequently uses graphic organizers in her plannning and she values graphic organizers as a practical tool as she explores interdisciplinary connections with her fellow teachers. Whatever your approach to interdisciplinary curriculum, graphic organizers are a valuable tool for planning, implementation, and evaluation. By highlighting the relationships among disciplines and the connections among concepts, graphic organizers promote interdisciplinary thinking and exciting new ways to design and implement curriculum.

● ●

References

Brandt, R. (1991). "On Interdisciplinary Curriculum: A Conversation with Heidi Hayes Jacobs." Educational Leadership, 49, (2), 24-26.
Gardner, H. (1983). *Frames of Mind*. New York: Basic Books.
Jacobs, H. (1989). *Interdisciplinary Curricum: Design and Implementation*. Alexandria, VA: Association for Supervision and Curriculum Development.
Kovalik, S. (1993). *Integrated Thematic Instruction: The Model*, 2nd ed. Oak Creek, AZ: Books for Educators
Roth, K. (1994). "Second Thoughts About Interdisciplinary Studies." *American Educator*, 18, 44-48.
Williams, J. & Reynolds, T. (1993). Courting Controversy: How to Build Inter-disciplinary Units. *Educational Leadership*, 50, (7), 13-15.

Questions & Answers

In which subjects and at which grade levels do graphic organizers work best?

Graphic organizers can be used in all subject areas and across all grade levels. Traditionally, they have been used most often in social studies and science at the high-school level. Today, elementary school teachers are also doing exciting work with graphic organizers in their teaching and in instruction planning. Both elementary and high school students currently use graphic organizers in language arts, social studies, science, math, the arts, technology, and in interdisciplinary situations.

Appendix A

Professional Resources

Bellanca, J. (1992; 1990). *Cooperative Think Tank: Graphic Organizers to Teach Thinking in the Cooperative Classroom*. Palatine, IL: Skylight Publishers.

Black, H., & Black, S. (1990). *Organizing Thinking: Graphic Organizers* (Book II). Pacific Grove, CA: Midwest Publications.

Bromley, K.D. (1991). *Webbing with Literature: Creating Story Maps with Children's Books*. Boston: Allyn & Bacon.

Heimlich, J.E., & Pittelman, S.D. (1986). *Semantic Mapping: Classroom Applications*. Newark, DE: International Reading Association.

Margulies, N. (1991). *Mapping Innerspace*. Tucson: Zephyr Press.

Moore, C.W., Readence, J.E., & Rickelman, R.J. (1989). *Prereading Activities for Content Area Reading and Learning*, Second Edition. Newark, DE: International Reading Association.

Parks, S., & Black, H. (1989). *Organizing Thinking: Graphic Organizers, Book I*. Pacific Grove, CA: Midwest Publications.

Pehrsson, R.S., & Denner, P.R. (1989). *Semantic Organizers: A Study Strategy for Special Needs Learners*. Rockville, MD: Aspen.

Seeley, A., & Soper, V. (1990). *Semantic Mapping: Prior Knowledge + Text*. Grand Rapids, MI: Virginia J., Inc.

Thelen, J. (1976). *Improving Reading in Science*. Newark, DE: International Reading Association.

Wycoff, J. (1991). *Mindmapping: Your Personal Guide to Exploring Creativity and Problem Solving*. New York: Berkley Books.

Software

Inspiration 4.0: The Easiest Way to Brainstorm and Write. Portland, OR: Inspiration Software, Inc. (2920 SW Dolph Ct., Suite 3, 97219; 1- 800-877-4292). IBM and MAC versions.

Kid Pix. San Rafael, CA: Borderbund Software, Inc. (17 Paul Drive., 94903-2101). IBM and MAC compatible.

The Semantic Mapper. Gainesville, FL: Teacher Support Software. (1035 NW 57th St., 32605-4486; 1-800-228-2871). MAC compatible.

Visuals

CP Graphic Organizers (1994). Elizabethtown, NJ: Continental Press. This is a set of laminated posters (24" x 37") that includes 12 of the most common graphic organizer formats.

Appendix B

Sample Graphic Organizer Patterns

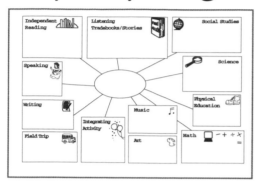

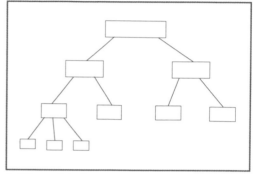

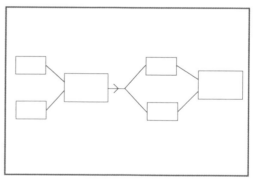

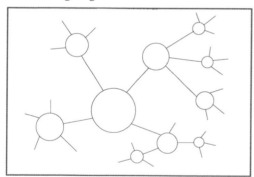

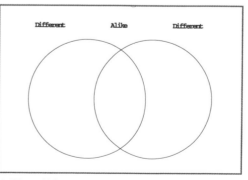

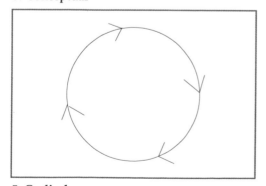

1. Planning Organizer

2. Hierarchical

3. Conceptual

4. Sequential

5. Cyclical

6. Venn Diagram

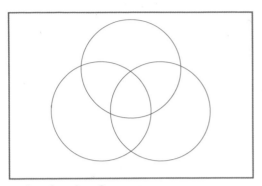

7. Overlapping Concepts

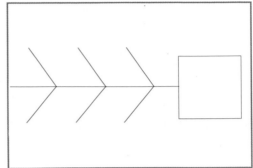

8. Cause-Effect

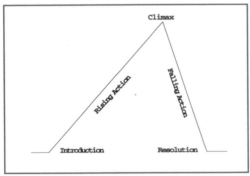

9. Plot Diagram

4362